The Foodie Bar™ Way

ONE MEAL. LOTS OF OPTIONS. EVERYONE'S HAPPY.

Timaree Hagenburger, MPH, RD, EP-C

Kathryn Mayo & Scot Hagenburger
Photography

The Nutrition Professor
LOVE THE FOOD THAT LOVES YOU BACK™

WWW.THENUTRITIONPROFESSOR.COM

Copyright © 2016 by Timaree Hagenburger

Photography © 2016 by Kathryn Mayo & Scot Hagenburger

Designed by Stephanie Faiferek

All rights reserved.

www.thenutritionprofessor.com

ISBN 978-0-9969062-0-3
Library of Congress Control Number: 2015917368
Printed in China.

I dedicate this book to my students (former and future). May The Foodie Bar™ Way enable you to find a happy place in your kitchen and experience phenomenal health, as you celebrate life, connection and food that truly "loves you back!"

Table of Contents

Introduction

Breakfast Bars

Meal Bars

Dessert Bars

More Recipes

A LETTER FROM THE NUTRITION PROFESSOR

Thank you for purchasing this book and congratulations on deciding to explore an approach to nourishing yourself and your family that is delicious, fun and inclusive! I am thrilled to begin to share my life's work with you in this way.

I want to invite you into my world, the real world of being a mom with way too many jobs and responsibilities. While there never seems to be enough time and there always seems to be too many tasks, I am committed to feeding my family the most nutrient dense food possible, staying within our budget and time constraints and also keeping everyone happy.

The Foodie Bar™ Way is how I do it...I love getting my family to eat food that loves them back, and turn the complainers into cheerleaders! "Really Mom? Dessert Nachos for breakfast? Yippee!" The Foodie Bar™ Way is my secret strategy that I want to share with everyone. In fact, my dream is for people to have "Cook2Gethers" (pg13) and spread the Foodie Bar™ Way throughout their communities and the world!

My kitchen is my "happy place"... I want it to be your happy place, too -- a place to relax and have fun! I have done the heavy lifting for you by putting together an array of ideas that will allow you to customize familiar meals with ingredients that "love you back!" Set out the options you find in the Foodie Bars™ and everyone can assemble the combination that's just right for them. You'll see how foods that are the very best for us fill the table and their plates, while the disease-promoting choices are crowded out!

Nourishing food is soooooo much more than "fuel" or "medicine" -- it is life and joy. It can give you energy, strength and peace. When you get it right, you'll feel better in your own skin. That is how I want you to approach food, to eat with the goal of feeling energized afterward and to truly "love the food that loves you back." I don't want you to diet or count calories, grams of protein, carbohydrate or fat. (This is precisely why you won't find the nutritional analysis for any of the recipes.) I just want you to start with a few deep breaths and enjoy every bite, until you aren't hungry anymore or the food doesn't taste amazing anymore. Like a little kid who leaves half a cookie, not because it wasn't delicious, just because she wasn't hungry anymore.

Honor your body's innate sense of hunger and fullness, along with the accompanying cues, and provide the very best options possible for yourself and your family. I want you to live your life and not to obsess about food—keep it in its place! Simply ask the question, "Is this going to help me become a better version of myself?"

You can and will do this. With The Foodie Bar™ Way, you'll be able to take care of yourself and your family's nutritional needs and even teach this approach to your kids and their kids. You will learn how to always have options and create a foundation upon which you can continually expand, branch out by using different ingredients and new flavor combinations, all while making memories AND having FUN!

With sincere gratitude,

Timaree

Every bite, every sip, every step and every thought... is a choice. Choose with intention and celebrate becoming a better version of yourself!

WHY THE FOODIE BAR™ WAY?

Life is crazy, so we all need to be at our best, mentally and physically, and we need options!

- We need options for food that makes us feel good from the inside out – "Love the Food that Loves You Back"™

- We need cooking skills, to save money, time and ensure that we are eating whole foods that taste amazing.

- We need options so that we can make little tweaks and don't get bored, while getting needed nutrients from a variety of sources.

- We need options that are inclusive to bring people together around the table, all ages, with allergies, intolerances, certain likes and dislikes.

- We need a "safe" way to branch out to trying new ingredients and flavors, while starting in a comfortable place with familiar favorites.

- We need quick and simple options sometimes, and more complex ones for special occasions.

- Life is too short to eat crummy food that makes you feel sick, sluggish or bloated afterwards!

- Life is too long to turn our bodies into toxic waste dumps, wrought with inflammation, clogged vessels and struggling organs.

- We need options that we enjoy and support the best versions of ourselves so that we can fulfill our potential!

The Foodie Bar™ Way enables you to choose what works for you!

Figure out where you are right now, in terms of time, money, your confidence in the kitchen, who you are eating/cooking with or if you are feeding yourself or the whole neighborhood... Then, be as adventurous as you'd like, cooking several recipes in a single day or working little by little over several days. From a simple Oatmeal Foodie Bar™ for one, to serving guests a Pasta Foodie Bar™ at a wedding reception (we did this!), The Foodie Bar™ Way is here for you and will meet you where you are!

The Foodie Bar™ Way is more than a cookbook, it is a movement!

Instead of friends and families being divided over what to eat, The Foodie Bar™ Way is about being united. Bringing us together around the table to share one meal, with lots of options, so that everyone's happy.

HOW TO USE THIS BOOK

Since you are considering new possibilities in the kitchen, possibly honing some cooking skills and broadening your taste preferences on YOUR TERMS... I invite you to explore this book in any way that makes sense to you!

- Why not start with the dessert bars? (These recipes are so amazing that you can actually have "dessert" for breakfast!)

- Find a familiar favorite (such as pizza or fried rice) and have fun setting up a Foodie Bar™ and making a version that loves you back!

- Decide on a few "Go-To Recipes" 🔘 since they can be used in multiple Foodie Bars™, and plan your week of meals around those, either preparing them throughout the week or during a mini "cook-a-thon" (a weekend afternoon might work best).

- Make double or triple batches of a few "Freezer-Friendly" ❄ recipes to save time and effort in the future, so you'll be able to set up a Foodie Bar™, even when you are super busy.

- Take a family vote to choose two Foodie Bars™ this week, then divide the prep among family members.

- Short on time and nothing in the freezer? Be sure to have "Basic Bar" ingredients on hand for a few Foodie Bars™ on the fly!

- Thumb through the pages until a specific picture catches your eye and go for it! The index will let you know which Foodie Bars™ incorporate that recipe.

- Use the INDEX! Look up an ingredient that you have on hand, (e.g. asparagus) to find out which bars and recipes feature that ingredient! Then you'll have several ideas for some extra variety during the week!

- If you love to experiment in the kitchen, and rarely stick to a recipe, have fun checking out all of the Foodie Bar™ options and then let your imagination run wild, being sure to jot down your creative additions in the designated areas of the book…

- Want some company in the kitchen? Invite a few friends over and cook side-by-side to prepare food to take home and enjoy all week. Choose a "**Cook2Gether**" Foodie Bar™ and decide on the options that suit taste preferences, including a few that are outside of your comfort zone, but you find intriguing. Each person can have a designated item or recipe to contribute, can shop on their own and depending on how much time you have, might want to do some preparation in advance. Or, you may decide to shop together as a group. During your actual Cook2Gether, either cook and eat together or cook together and divide up the food to take home!

- Choose a Foodie Bar™ for your next party or potluck and go through the list of items under "Basic Bar" or "Raising the Bar", assigning one or more items to each member of your group.

Attention all parents and grandparents: The Foodie Bar™ Way is excellent for simultaneously encouraging autonomy and fostering team work! For the prep, items can be assigned to each family member to work on with a partner or independently, then everyone comes together to work as a team to set out the variety of options and enjoy the Foodie Bar™ meal!

The most important thing to remember, is **HAVE FUN!** Keep your sense of humor intact as you enjoy this hands-on adventure! The Foodie Bar™ Way creates a mindset shift. You'll look at your food options with a completely different perspective. Now, you'll see one possibility after another...

SETTING YOURSELF UP IN THE KITCHEN
SUCCESS BY DESIGN!

Life is hard enough, why not use these two EASY, and powerful techniques to dramatically improve your experience in the kitchen!

SET UP A PREP SMART AREA

I had the honor of being able to attend a Healthy Kitchen, Healthy Lives Conference held at the Culinary Institute of America at Greystone, and I clearly remember one of their lead Culinary Faculty, Bill Briwa, explain that when he observes **students with messy preparation areas,** they:

- get frazzled easily and make mistakes with ingredients
- often feel more anxious and stressed
- their food ends up looking "messy/ sloppy"...not FUN!

Being surrounded with clutter leads to wasting time and makes everything more difficult, no matter the situation! So, whether you have a tiny kitchen in your apartment or are cooking for several hundred in a commercial facility, taking a minute or two organize your preparation area will set you up for success!

Move ingredients from one area (to be used) to another area (already used), so that you don't end up adding an ingredient twice (e.g. baking powder, baking soda, etc.). A scrap bowl saves times and extra mess. Use a wet washcloth underneath your cutting board if it seems to be a bit "shifty". Have pepper, spices, veggie broth, ingredient bowls - small (ceramic or glass) and larger (stainless), at your fingertips.

TEST DRIVE A DIFFERENT PERSPECTIVE

Changing your mindset about prepping and cooking can make a huge difference. It is about making a little shift in your thinking...

- **Instead of:** "Cutting up my own produce is such a hassle."
  How about: "I save a lot of money each year cutting up my produce."

- **Instead of:** "Prepping produce makes a big mess in the kitchen."
  How about: "A scrap bowl makes prep go faster and cleanup easier."

- **Instead of:** "Chopping and slicing is tedious."
  How about: "I can relax when I am chopping and slicing because I can focus on working with my knife and block everything else out."

Invite others to help... (when it makes sense)
Turn off the TV...
Put on your favorite music...
Organize a Prep Smart area (see pictures)...
Relax and HAVE FUN preparing food that is going to nourish your body!

Ingredients to be used

Used ingredients

FRESH VS FROZEN

WHEN FRESH IS BEST!

While local fresh fruits and veggies are great (your own backyard, neighbor's backyard or Farmers' Market), supermarkets often import fresh produce from far away - which can mean:

- long travel time (loss of nutrients)
- picked unripe (lower levels of nutrients)
- expensive (especially if out of season)

FRUITS AND VEGGIES TO PURCHASE FRESH:

Salad greens, parsley, red onions, scallions, garlic, asparagus*, sweet potatoes, eggplant, avocado, jicama, snow peas, snap beans, carrots, cucumber, zucchini, cabbage (all types), cherry tomatoes*, Brussels*, bok choy, celery, red bell peppers, mushrooms, pomegranates*, persimmons*, grapes*, strawberries*, lemons, limes, oranges, apples, pears, kiwi, melons*, bananas, stone fruit*, broccoli, cauliflower
*when in season

FROZEN PRODUCE — WHEN IS IT SMART TO HEAD TO THE FREEZER SECTION?

Frozen fruit and veggies could be the best option for you because:

- They were picked at their peak ripeness and typically processed within a few hours, so they retain an amazingly high amount of nutrients! (Most people don't realize this and assume that "fresh" is always better.)
- They are ridiculously convenient: at your fingertips when you are ready to set up a Foodie Bar™ or recipe
- Easy to use: No cleaning or chopping needed - just cut the bag open and shake out the amount you want (keep the rest frozen).
- No worry about them going bad within the week (some will last for a month or more in the freezer).
- Shorter cooking times: Veggies are blanched before they are frozen, so

they don't need to be cooked very much (if at all, once thawed) – Don't over cook them – you want vibrant colors and good texture – not mushy!

Berries can mold so quickly that I RARELY purchase them fresh (only strawberries when in season) – so my freezer is always packed with an assortment of frozen berries.

FRUITS AND VEGGIES TO PURCHASE FROZEN:

Spinach, kale, chard, collard greens, corn, peas, berries (raspberries, blackberries, blueberries, cranberries and strawberries), cherries, mango, pineapple, broccoli, edamame (organic)

ORGANIC OR BUST?! – NOT YET!

While it would be fantastic if all farmers switched to organic methods of farming, that is not going to happen overnight. In the meantime, we are faced with choices in the supermarket and Farmers' Market. Here is my advice:

- Buy organic when you can (better for consumers, farm workers and the environment), BUT – Never let organic be a barrier to eating fruits and vegetables – conventional produce is always better than no fruits and/or vegetables!
- Don't assume that organic means more expensive – at my local supermarket, organic cauliflower is routinely less expensive than conventionally grown cauliflower
- Refer to the Environmental Working Group's Dirty Dozen and Clean 15 (free online resource, updated each year) to prioritize your organic produce purchases
- Organic means Non-GMO (important for soy and corn products)
- The majority of pesticide exposure (80-90%) comes from animal products due to bio-accumulation (fish, chicken, pork, cow's milk, cheese, butter, eggs, beef)
- When shopping at the Farmers' Market - ask each farmer/vendor if they spray with pesticides, as many don't but have not gone through the hassle (and expense) of getting certified as "organic"
- Check out local CSAs (Community Supported Agriculture), as many are exclusively organic and deliver boxes of produce to your doorstep!

HOW TO MAKE YOUR FOOD, ESPECIALLY PRODUCE, LAST LONGER!

The two most important factors in determining how long your food will last are temperature and moisture. We have a second refrigerator in our garage because I cook so much from scratch and want to have options at my family members' fingertips throughout the week. I also have children who open the fridge, while they are trying to figure out "what they feel like eating"... so I use the garage fridge for food that goes bad the quickest (our salad greens for sure) or that I need to last the longest (a second container of Quick Pasta Sauce, Cheezie Sauce, Cauliflower Lentil filling, Seasoned Lentils or cooked sweet potatoes for my lunch salads, etc.). On several occasions, when I have hesitated or forgotten to move something into the garage fridge, I have discovered moldy food – which drives me BATTY! I work so hard to make wonderful food, I hate to see it get wasted.

An interesting tip is to keep your fridge fairly full to optimize energy usage, since less space in between items, means less air that will rush out when the door is opened and less space for new (warmer) air to rush in and need to be cooled. Even simply keeping full water jugs can help.

I love using my freezer whenever possible. We have invested in a stand alone freezer for our garage. I prefer the upright style, not chest-type, which I find much more difficult to keep organized. That freezer has EASILY been one of the smartest purchases we have ever made. I keep it full of sauces, spreads (including hummus), cooked beans, nuts, flours, frozen fruits and vegetables, granola, pancakes, waffles, bread, (including whole grain pitas, Lavash, bagels, etc.), veggie burgers, citrus juice and zest, ginger root, homemade popsicles and fruited ice cubes, grains (e.g. raw and cooked brown/wild/red/black/purple rice, oats, quinoa, barley, bulgur, millet etc.), seeds (e.g. sunflower, flax, sesame seeds, etc.). A full freezer not only ensures that we have many available food options, but it also protects the contents in the event that the freezer loses power, as a full freezer can keep most items frozen for twice as long as one that is half full.

When it comes to moisture - too much can lead to quick deterioration/mold/decay (especially with berries or greens), but too little moisture can lead to dried out, wilted produce. General rules – don't wash/rinse produce until just before you plan to use it and shop frequently for your most perishable items. I have also provided some specific guidance below.

Apples: Ripen on the counter and then move to the fridge in a loose bag to extend their life. Remove any decaying apples quickly, as the old saying "It only takes one bad apple to ruin the bunch" is true! Cut apples will brown quickly when exposed to air, though a squeeze of citrus high in vitamin C (lemon, orange, pineapple, lime) can help.

Apricots/Nectarines/Peaches/Plums: Ripen on the counter (or in a paper bag* if you want to speed up the process). Be sure to check fruits often as they tend to go from unripe, to perfectly ripe, to mushy/moldy quite quickly.

Asparagus: If I have room in the fridge, I will put the bunch of asparagus in a glass/vase with water (as I would flowers) and loosely cover with plastic wrap/plastic bag. Otherwise, I will keep the asparagus in a produce bag, unwashed, in the crisper drawer.

Avocados: Ripen on the counter (or in a paper bag* if you want to speed up the process). Be sure to check avocados often, as they can go from unripe, to perfectly ripe, to soft and moldy before you know it. As soon as they yield to gentle pressure, you can move them into the fridge, where they should last for a few more days. Depending on how you plan to use them, if you mash them with some lemon or lime juice, the mixture can be frozen for later when making guacamole or dip.

Bananas: Ripen on the counter. To slow the process, tightly wrap the stem in plastic wrap. When you move perfectly ripe bananas to the fridge, their skins will darken, but the flesh will stay firm for a few more days. Peel over-ripened bananas and put them in a zip-top freezer bag (either whole or cut into chunks). Having frozen bananas at your fingertips is a must for smoothies, breads, desserts and more!

Beets: Remove the greens right away, cut them off where they meet the beet root, and the roots should last for at least several weeks in a plastic produce bag in the crisper drawer.

Blackberries, Blueberries and Raspberries: These berries do not continue to ripen after being picked and will mold quite quickly, especially when exposed to moisture. In fact, I almost never purchase fresh blackberries, blueberries or raspberries, as they seem to mold on the way home from the market! In my opinion, frozen is the way to go! If you really need to buy fresh for a particular recipe, carefully check for mold and/or moisture at the market, remove any soft berries as soon as you get them home, store in their original well ventilated plastic container, don't rinse/wash them until you are ready to use them and use them right away!

Broccoli: Get broccoli into the refrigerator as soon as possible after purchasing. Keep unwashed, in a loosely closed produce bag, so that air can circulate - in the crisper drawer, when possible.

Brussels sprouts: Refrigerate in a plastic bag for up to 3 days, don't wash until you are ready to use them.

Cabbage: Whole head of cabbage lasts longer than packages of shredded cabbage. Keep head in plastic bag in the crisper drawer. Only cut off the amount you need, wrap the remaining piece tightly in plastic wrap. Rinse the piece you plan to use and chop/shred/slice/dice away!

Cantaloupe and Papaya: Ripen on counter, but keep an eye on them as they tend to go bad quickly if the room temperature in the kitchen is above 72F. Refrigerate cut fruit right way, either tightly wrapped (for half or quarter of whole fruit) or in an airtight container (for fruit cut into chunks).

Carrots: In my experience, the baby carrots get slimy quickly, so I buy "regular" carrots, and keep them in the crisper drawer in the bag they came in. Don't scrub them until ready to use, leave the peel on to maximize the nutrients they provide.

Cauliflower: Store, unwashed, in a plastic bag in the crisper drawer of fridge. If brown spots begin to appear, cut those off unless they are deep and the surface is slimy (it has gone bad).

Celery: To maximize lifespan, store in crisper drawer, in a plastic bag or wrapped in damp paper towel and then aluminum foil. If the celery gets limp, slice and place in a bowl of ice water before using.

Chia: Chia seeds can be kept at room temperature, in a dark cabinet, away from moisture and heat.

Coconut: I store unsweetened, raw coconut flakes in my freezer.

Corn: While frozen corn can last for months, fresh corn is quite perishable and should be enjoyed within a day of purchasing it. Corn tends to go bad from the tip down, so it is important to peel the husk and silk away from the top and see if it is discolored or moldy. Keep it in a bag in the crisper drawer.

Cranberries: Buy frozen or fresh and toss the whole bag into the freezer, unwashed. Rinse the amount you need when you are ready to use them.

Cucumbers: Whole cucumbers will last longer than when cut. Store in a plastic bag in the crisper drawer. Wrap cut cucumbers tightly or place a damp paper towel on cut ends in a bag.

Dates: I pit the dates (I like to buy the Medjool variety), when I get them home, for 2 reasons: 1) to avoid a stray pit, as it only takes one to ruin your recipe and potentially your food processor or blender and 2) to find and throw away any dates with black powdery mold. I put the pitted dates in a heavy-duty quart size zip-top bag, and store them in the fridge (will last for months) or freezer (will last for years).

Eggplant: Store in produce bag in crisper drawer of fridge. Rinse and cut right before you plan to use it.

Flax seeds: I keep my whole flax seeds in the freezer, as they contain essential fats that are heat sensitive. Every week to 10 days, I grind a mason jar's worth to keep in the fridge, using my flax grinder (an inexpensive coffee grinder that I only use for flax).

Garlic: Keep head of garlic together, with skin attached, and store at room temperature, in a container or mesh bag with good air circulation (I use a clay pot with holes in it), avoid plastic bags. Only refrigerate peeled cloves, and wrap them tightly.

Ginger: Store, unpeeled, in a brown bag in the crisper drawer. Can also tightly wrap in plastic and freeze.

Greens - Kale, chard, collard and beet greens: I rinse these greens and then immediately plunge them into a large bowl of ice water (to remove the dust/dirt/debris), let them rest there for a few minutes to a few hours. If I am super busy in the kitchen, I will add more ice to keep the water cool. Then, I'll spin them in my salad spinner, roll greens in paper towel and place in a clean produce bag in the crisper drawer. You could also treat them like cut flowers (water filled vase in fridge), similar to herbs or asparagus if you have the space, but were not ready to use them for a few days. Whenever possible, it is best to buy fresh greens as close to when you plan to use them as possible.

Herbs (fresh): Depending on how quickly you need to use them – I will store my fresh herbs in one of two ways. If I don't plan to use the entire amount for several days, I will put the bunch in a glass/vase with water (as I would flowers) and loosely cover with plastic wrap/plastic bag. When I prepare my salad mix for the week, I soak parsley and any other fresh herbs in a large bowl of ice water (to remove the dust/dirt/debris), spin them in my salad spinner, then roll them in paper towel and put that roll into a clean produce bag in my crisper drawer. Fresh herbs can also be cleaned and chopped, then frozen in ice cube trays, with water covering, if adding to a soup, blended dressing or another recipe which does not require a crisp texture (unlike a salad, for which you would want to use fresh herbs).

Jicama: Keep unwashed, uncut jicama in a cool, dry place for a week or so. Once cut and peeled, wrap tightly and refrigerate, if you are not going to use it immediately.

Kiwi: Ripen on the counter, transfer to fridge when they yield to gentle pressure.

Lemons and Limes: You can freeze whole, or freeze zest and juice in ice cube trays – in 1-2 Tablespoon amounts, depending on how much liquid your ice cube trays hold. Once frozen, transfer the cubes to a heavy duty zip-top bag for easier storage.

Lettuce: To serve a salad with crisp lettuce, keep unwashed lettuce in a loose produce bag. An hour or so before you plan to prepare the salad, rinse lettuce in cool water and roll in dry paper towel, then place into produce bag and refrigerate until ready to assemble the salad.

Mangoes: Ripen on the counter (or in a paper bag* if you want to speed up the process). Be sure to check mangoes, so they don't over-ripen. I love buying frozen cubed mango, as it is extremely convenient, and picked at their peak of ripeness and frozen within hours, maximizing the nutrient levels.

Mushrooms: Get mushrooms quickly into a paper bag and place them in the back of the fridge, as they will last longer in paper and retain the highest level of nutrients when kept consistently cold.

Nuts/Seeds/Whole Grains/Whole Grain Flours: Keep them in the freezer!!!

Onions: Store onions whole, with outer skin intact, in a dark, cool area/cabinet (not next to your stove or oven), away from potatoes. If you have the space, you can experiment with tying each onion off in the legs of panty-hose and hanging them, for optimal air circulation. Store cut onions in tightly sealed glass containers.

Pears: Ripen on the counter (or in a paper bag* if you want to speed up the process). Be sure to check pears often as they tend to go from unripe, to perfectly ripe, to mushy/moldy quite quickly.

Peppers: Will last longest if kept whole and unwashed, in the crisper drawer of fridge. Once cut, wrap tightly and use soon.

Pineapple: Can store on counter for 1-2 days, but will not ripen any further after being picked, and should be stored in the fridge to last longer.

Potatoes: Store potatoes in a dark, cool area/cabinet (not next to your stove or oven), away from onions.

Salad mix/greens: I keep my salad greens in the garage refrigerator (stays cold because the door is rarely opened) with paper towel in between layers to absorb excess moisture.

Scallions (green onions): Keep unwashed scallions in a plastic produce bag in crisper drawer of fridge. Once chopped, will last for a few days in an air-tight container in back of the fridge.

Squash (hard winter): Uncut and unwashed in a cool, dark area (can last for 1-3 months), if cut or sliced, will keep in refrigerator for 2-4 days in an air-tight container.

Strawberries: Do not continue to ripen after being picked and will mold quite quickly, especially when exposed to moisture. Store unwashed strawberries in a plastic container, being careful not to crowd the fruit and removing any soft/molding berries right away.

Tomatoes: Best kept at room temperature, stem side down (to prevent air from entering and moisture from leaving).

Watermelon: Will not ripen on counter, highest amount of nutrients (esp. lycopene) before being refrigerated. Refrigerate cut watermelon right way, either tightly wrapped (for half or quarter of whole melon) or in an airtight container (for chunks of watermelon).

Zucchini: Store in a plastic produce bag in the crisper drawer of your fridge. Do not wash until you are ready to use.

*I write "PEARS/NECTARINES/ MANGOES/AVOCADOS in here!" in very large letters on the front of the paper bag, to remind myself that something wonderful is ripening in there. The "out of sight, out of mind" phenomenon has previously resulted in moldy fruit and much frustration.

OTHER TIPS AND TRICKS FOR MAKING FOOD LAST LONGER:

_____

_____

_____

_____

THE MOST IMPORTANT COOKING TOOL

If I had to choose a single cooking tool that was most important, I'd have to say a "good" knife.

While knives can get to be ridiculously expensive ($500+), and are often sold in sets, you really only need 2 knives, and some practice, to be quite the ninja in the kitchen!

HOW TO PICK OUT A KNIFE:

Large knife – You will want to have a Chef's knife or a Santoku (chef's knife meets cleaver). When you hold this knife in your hand, it should feel solid and a bit heavy. My favorite is a 8" or 10" Chef's knife, though you might be more comfortable with a 6" Chef's knife. My second favorite is my 7" Santoku.

You will also want a small paring knife. Simply find one that feels good in your hand and able to be sharpened (do not buy any knife described as "ever-sharp" – no sharpening needed).

Sharp knives reduce the likelihood of cutting yourself – as the knife will slice easily rather than you having to exert a lot of pressure and increase the chance that the knife could slip. If you don't feel comfortable sharpening your own knives, the butchers at most local markets will sharpen your knives for a nominal cost (sometimes for free).

Hold the knife so that you have the most control (see picture).
Position your fingers of the hand holding the food so that it is practically impossible to get cut (see picture). If you keep your fingers away from the blade, you can't get cut!!!

A FEW MORE TIPS ABOUT KNIVES...

Don't ever put knives in the sink, especially in soapy water – as someone may not realize that the knife is in there, reach in and get cut!

Carefully wash and dry the knife you are using as soon as you are done, to keep them in good shape. They will stay sharpest in a butcher block or attached to a magnetic strip mounted to the wall.

Stay focused when you are using a knife, cut away from your body and don't try to catch a knife if it is falling, it is not worth getting cut!

HOW TO HOLD A KNIFE

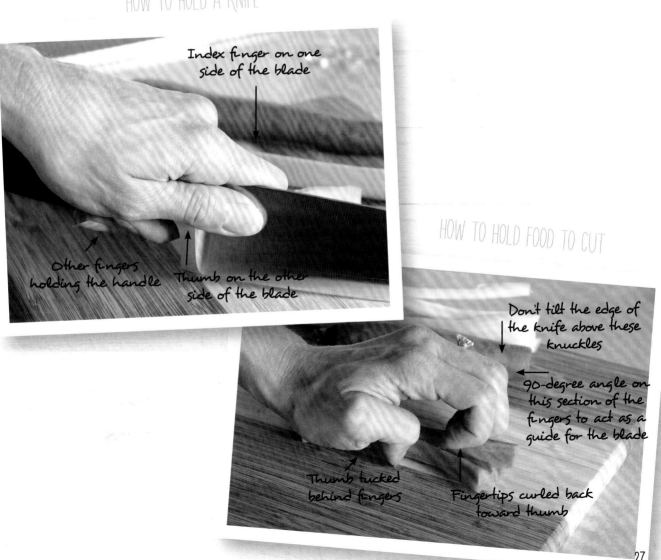

Index finger on one side of the blade

Other fingers holding the handle

Thumb on the other side of the blade

HOW TO HOLD FOOD TO CUT

Don't tilt the edge of the knife above these knuckles

90-degree angle on this section of the fingers to act as a guide for the blade

Thumb tucked behind fingers

Fingertips curled back toward thumb

A FEW WORDS ABOUT HEALTH AND HOPE

When I look out at my students, I see the real threat that they will be the first generation to live shorter lives than their parents. Not only are we sicker than ever before in history, we are getting sicker younger, and we are digging our graves with our knives and forks. While the statistics are staggering, this isn't just about numbers, it is personal. We all know someone who is struggling with a scary, chronic disease, like heart disease, hypertension, diabetes, Alzheimer's or cancer, which limits their freedom to fulfill their potential and celebrate life with those around them. It breaks my heart when a 19 year old student writes in her class journal about how her 48 year old mother died of a stroke in her arms.

It doesn't have to be that way! These chronic diseases are not inevitable! In fact, we now know that a great majority of these diseases are preventable and reversible for those willing to change how they nourish their bodies. If you have been told that your health destiny lies in your genes, rest assured, as you can begin to change the way your genes behave (e.g. turning cancer promoting genes "off" and cancer killing genes "on"). You can also leave behind strategies from the diet and weight loss industry, which only perpetuate the cycle of losing and re-gaining weight, negatively impact our happiness and overall mental health, and are particularly dangerous in terms of promoting diseases like cancer. Though many people tend to become comfortable being uncomfortable and resist change, I am forever hopeful, as some of us are ready to stand up for eating well and feeling great!

The simple approach that I have found to be amazingly effective, both personally and with my family, students and clients, is to choose plant-based whole foods. As Dr. Michael Greger describes, "As grown in nature, nothing good taken away and nothing bad added." While it seems too good to be true, I am humbled by the miraculous power of the body to respond to vegetables, fruits, legumes, whole grains, nuts and seeds. Their phytonutrients "phyt" (fight) for us in so many ways, including building and supporting a strong immune system to keep us healthy.

If I didn't see it with my own eyes, I wouldn't believe it. I am in awe as those who have struggled with debilitating pain and disease for years, experience dramatic improvements in their quality of life and physical health within days of transitioning to a whole food plant-based way of eating. I was recently brought to tears when I received a "thank you" email from a gentleman in his sixties who watched a televised version of my college nutrition class on cable, explaining that despite a diagnosis of Type 2 Diabetes, his HgbA1c had dropped into the normal range (5.3% for the past 2 years) since adopting this eating style. I was speechless when a student flagged me down on campus to tell me how her blood cholesterol plummeted into the normal range, her energy level shot through the roof and how good she feels, "I feel better in my own skin, just better being me." That is the best outcome that I could imagine, and I see it over and over. And if you are wondering, yes, the science backs this up. The benefits of embracing a whole food plant-based diet are real and the food tastes fantastic (and the wonderful options are nearly endless with The Foodie Bar™ Way to guide in you)!

Every bite you take is an opportunity to feel great and become a better version of yourself, strengthening your body, fortifying your blood, supporting your immune system and protecting your brain. Make every bite count! "Love the food that loves you back!™"

TAKING THE FOODIE BAR™ WAY OUT IN THE WORLD

RESTAURANTS... WHAT DO YOU SEE WHEN YOU LOOK AT THE MENU?

Not only will you gain confidence in the kitchen as you explore this book and Foodie Bar™ concept, but it can change your perspective on the power of choice when it comes to what you eat and drink "out in the world." This mindset shift might even impact how you view eating at restaurants, as you will no longer look at your choices as limited by the menu. Now, you'll view all dining experiences as an array of options. Instead of pre-set entrées, you'll see a variety of ingredients to combine in ways that best suit your taste preferences. When we have the choice, we enjoy nourishing our bodies and end up healthier, since we actually absorb more nutrients when you love what we are eating!

THE BEST POTLUCKS... EVER!

No more boring potlucks with five people bringing the same thing or one person burdened by coming up with a theme and how to organize it. Pick a Foodie Bar™ and divide up the components! One of my favorite potlucks is the Crazy Salad Foodie Bar™. For added excitement, you can even make one of the dressing recipes on the spot!

AN EASY WAY TO ORGANIZE OTHER RECIPES

The Foodie Bar™ Way will even help you organize and search for recipes. Now, you can think in terms of your favorite Foodie Bars™. Find an interesting pesto recipe online, in another cookbook or a magazine? Add it to your Pesto Foodie Bar™!

BREAKFAST BARS

Scramble Bar

Basic Bar

VEGETABLES TO SAUTE:

Red onion, thinly sliced or finely diced

Garlic, minced or pressed

Mixed vegetables (frozen)

Spinach, chopped (frozen or fresh)

(Add diced red onion to a dry pan over medium to medium-high heat, cooking until onions begin to brown, then add in garlic and cook for ~30 seconds, adding a few teaspoons of water/vegetable broth, if needed to prevent burning. Add in other vegetables, and cook until almost tender.)

WHILE VEGGIES ARE COOKING, PREPARE THE TOFU:

15 ounces organic tofu, extra firm – water packed – not silken*

(drained, pressed to remove excess water and crumbled/mashed with a fork)

MIX TOFU WITH:

½ teaspoon turmeric powder

½ teaspoon black pepper, ground

2 Tablespoons nutritional yeast flakes

(Add tofu to cooked vegetables and heat until warmed through and extra liquid has evaporated.)

TOPPING OPTIONS:

Avocado

Salsa (store bought)

Squeeze of lime juice

Salt/pepper (to taste)

Hot sauce (if desired)

MY OWN ADDITIONS OR IDEAS/RECIPES TO TRY:

_____

_____

34

Raising the Bar

ADDITIONAL OR ALTERNATIVE VEGETABLE OPTIONS:

Kale*, collard greens or chard, fresh or frozen, finely chopped*

Broccoli florets (fresh or frozen)

Carrot, finely grated

Zucchini, diced small

Sun-dried tomatoes

Beans, any variety (cooked from dry or canned and rinsed)

Chipotle in adobo* (remove seeds and add to pan with onion and garlic)

Roasted peppers (jarred)

Asparagus

ADDITIONAL TOPPING OPTIONS:

Homemade salsa (See Salsa Foodie Bar pg174)

Red/purple cabbage, shredded

Fresh cilantro, finely chopped

Jalapeño pepper, fresh or pickled

Tomato, diced small

Scallions, finely chopped

Fresh parsley, finely chopped

Olives, chopped very small

*SHOP SMART, PREP SMART, COOK SMART TIPS

* I pulse frozen greens (collards, spinach or kale) in my food processor in batches, until they are tiny pieces – but not liquefied. This ensures the fabulous greens don't get picked out and/or left on any-one's plate. I work in batches and am careful NOT to let the greens thaw out, as it works best when they are still very frozen. Otherwise, you'll end up with a puree/soup!
* Chipotle in adobo can be found canned or jarred in nearly every supermarket and adds a smoky fla-vor. The seeds in these roasted jalapeños are very spicy, so be sure to keep them out of your recipes if you don't like a lot of heat!

NEXT TIME I MAKE THIS FOODIE BAR, I WILL:

_____

_____

*SHOP SMART, PREP SMART, COOK SMART TIPS

* Buy refrigerated tofu either packed in water in a plastic tub or vacuum sealed. Do not use tofu labeled "silken" for this recipe, which is most often sold in a shelf stable aseptic carton/box, (think juice box).
* Use a variety of chopped leafy greens: kale, collard greens, spinach, mustard greens or chard.
* Serve on crisp romaine lettuce leaves for an alternative to tortillas.

Scrambled Tacos

Not only are these super tasty, they are also extremely economical and once made, will last in the fridge for several days and be enough to fill 20 tacos! Then, a satisfying meal can be ready in less than 5 minutes, any time of day! If you are a more traditional breakfast eater, make a batch of the filling and enjoy these at lunch or dinner.

INGREDIENTS

¾ cup red onion, thinly sliced or finely diced

1 Tablespoon garlic, minced or pressed

1 large carrot, finely grated

10 ounces kale*, fresh or frozen, finely chopped

15 ounces organic tofu, extra firm – water packed – not silken*

½ teaspoon turmeric powder

½ teaspoon sea salt, optional

½ teaspoon black pepper, ground

2 Tablespoons nutritional yeast flakes, optional

12 ounce jar of salsa

1 ½ cups black beans, cooked (or 15 ounce can of black beans, rinsed)

Optional, but wonderful toppings: avocado, cilantro, purple cabbage (finely sliced), hot sauce, salsa, pico de gallo, squeeze of fresh lime juice

PROCEDURE

1. Drain tofu from package, wrap in a clean dish towel or paper towels, and press out extra water. Transfer to a medium sized bowl, mash with a fork until crumbly, mix in turmeric, salt, pepper and nutritional yeast.

2. Heat pan over medium high and add the red onion, cooking until softened and lightly brown, 3-5 minutes. Add garlic and carrot, cook for 1-2 minutes, add chopped kale and cook for another 3-5 minutes.

3. Add tofu mixture, salsa, and black beans to veggies and cook for a few minutes until heated through and any extra liquid in pan has evaporated.

Oatmeal Bar

I EAT OATMEAL NEARLY EVERY WEEKDAY MORNING, SO TO KEEP IT INTERESTING, I CHANGE UP THE FRUIT AND SPICES. TO SAVE TIME, I MAKE A TRIPLE BATCH OF OATMEAL ON THE WEEKEND, SO THAT I CAN PORTION IT OUT INTO 5 CONTAINERS AND GRAB ONE EACH MORNING.

Basic Bar

INGREDIENTS:

¾ cup old-fashioned oatmeal

2-3 teaspoons chia seeds

Cook for 5 minutes in ~1 3/4 cups of water - use more water (up to 2 1/2 cups) if you'll be eating it later or the next day.

STIR-IN OPTIONS:

Apple, cut into small pieces or grated

Banana slices cut in half or quarters

Raisins

Cinnamon

MY OWN ADDITIONS OR IDEAS/RECIPES TO TRY:

_____

_____

Raising the Bar

INGREDIENTS:

1/2 cup steel-cut oats

2-3 teaspoons chia seeds

(cooked for ~30 minutes or until tender, in 2 cups of water)

TOPPINGS:

Walnuts, Almond, Pecans, Pistachios, Hazelnuts, Peanuts

Granola (See Granola Foodie Bar pg46 or Scot's Granola pg48)

Flax seeds, ground

Hemp seeds

Coconut

STIR-IN OPTIONS:

Berries: Blueberries, Strawberries, Raspberries, Blackberries, Cranberries

Kiwi

Mango

Pears

Pineapple

Peach/Nectarine

Figs, Dates, Dried Apricots, Goji Berries

Citrus – Orange, Lemon, Tangerine

Grapefruit sections (remove membrane and cut into small pieces)

Pumpkin, Butternut Squash, Acorn Squash

Nut Butter (1 Tablespoon): almond, peanut, cashew, sunflower seed

Pumpkin Pie Spice pg284

Chai Spice Blend pg282

NEXT TIME I MAKE THIS FOODIE BAR, I WILL:

_____

_____

Pistachio-Kissed Blackberry Pear Oatmeal

Not only is this recipe delicious, but it is gorgeous! You will feel like you are at a spa, as you dive in! With fiber supplements flying off the shelves, many people forget that choosing food sources of fiber is not only more economical, but your taste buds will be thrilled! This recipe combines 3 super sources of fiber: pears, blackberries and oats. Eating smart tastes great and feels wonderful!

INGREDIENTS

½ cup uncooked old fashioned oats

1 teaspoon chia seeds

1 cup water

1 teaspoon ground cinnamon

½ ripe pear*, diced

½ cup blackberries (fresh or frozen*)

2 Tablespoons crushed pistachios*, divided

PROCEDURE

1. Bring water and a dash of salt to a boil, add oats mixed with the chia seeds, stir well, and simmer for 5 minutes.

2. Off the heat, stir in cinnamon and pear.

3. Spoon half of the mixture into a bowl, top with half of the blackberries and a Tablespoon of pistachios.

4. Repeat with another layer of oatmeal, the remaining blackberries and sprinkle with pistachios.

5. Take a second to admire your beautiful creation, then enjoy every, single bite!

Chai Spiced Oatmeal with Apple, Chia and Goji Berries

I like to make my oatmeal for the week on Sunday evening (tripling this recipe), while cleaning up the kitchen from dinner. Once the apples are chopped, there is very little "work" involved, and then I have delicious breakfast waiting for me each morning! This particular recipe only has a few ingredients, but has turned into one of my favorites.

INGREDIENTS

2 ½ cups water

~¾ cups old fashioned rolled oats

1 Tablespoon chia seeds

1 apple, with skin, diced

1-2 Tablespoons Goji berries*, dried

¼–½ teaspoons Chai Spice Blend pg282

Topping (add right before serving)

1 Tablespoon ground flax seed* or chopped walnuts*

PROCEDURE

1. Bring water to a boil and then add oats and slowly sprinkle in chia seeds and Chai Spice Blend, mixing well with a whisk, so that the chia seeds don't clump together.

2. Cook for 5 minutes.

3. The mixture will have quite a bit of extra liquid, but don't worry, simply add the apple, cover, turn off the heat and let it sit.

4. You can add the Gogi berries at the end with the apples or while the oatmeal is cooking.

*SHOP SMART, PREP SMART, COOK SMART TIPS:

* Goji berries can be quite expensive, so organic raisins or blueberries can be substituted.
* Keep ground flax seeds and walnuts in freezer to maintain the highest amount of nutrients.

*SHOP SMART, PREP SMART, COOK SMART TIPS:

* DON'T PEEL YOUR APPLES! Much of the amazing health-promoting nutrients are found in and just under the skin, so simply core the apples and you are ready to go!
* I like a bit of "crunch" in my apple, but if you would like your apple to have a softer texture, add it halfway through the cooking time or shred/grate the apple instead of dicing it.
* You can also substitute steel cut oats, with a ratio of 1 cup oats to 4 cups water, and increase cooking time to ~30 minutes.

Oatmeal on the Fly

While I need a nourishing breakfast that is ready when I am, I also enjoy a variety of flavors and like to minimize the number of pots and pans to clean. All of this adds up to my "Oatmeal on the Fly". I typically make this recipe for our week on Sunday evening, while doing dishes from dinner. My basic recipe works well for making it ahead, as there is plenty of liquid for the oatmeal to absorb and it does not get too firm in the fridge during the week and can be flavored differently for each day!

INGREDIENTS

7 ½ cups water

~2 ⅔ cups old fashioned rolled oats*

3 Tablespoons chia seeds

3 apples, with skin, diced or shredded

Spice blends of your choice

Additional fruit (see ideas below)

Nuts or seeds (see ideas below)

PROCEDURE

1. Bring water to a boil and then add oats and slowly sprinkle in chia seeds, mixing well with a whisk, so that the chia seeds don't clump together.

2. Cook for 5 minutes. The mixture will have quite a bit of extra liquid, but don't worry, simply add the apple* and spices, cover, turn off the heat and let it sit on the stove.

3. Divide the cooked oatmeal into several bowls and experiment with different flavor combinations:

    blueberries (frozen) and apple pie spice (sprinkle with almonds before serving)

    bananas and Chai Spice Blend pg282 (sprinkle with pecans before serving)

    pumpkin, cranberries and Pumpkin Pie Spice pg284 (sprinkle with walnuts or pecans before serving)

    mango and cinnamon (sprinkle with hemp seeds before serving)

    mixed frozen berries and cinnamon (sprinkle with pepitas before serving)

    Let your imagination take over…

4. Transfer your flavorful oatmeal creations to appropriate containers for each day of the week. When cool, you can sprinkle with some freshly ground flaxseed, if desired.

Granola Bar

THIS BAR IS ALL ABOUT MAKING YOUR OWN GRANOLA (NOT GRANOLA BARS). I THINK THAT YOU WILL BE PRETTY EXCITED WITH THE RESULT, AS MOST STORE-BOUGHT GRANOLA IS FULL OF OIL AND REFINED SUGAR. MY RECIPES HAVE NEITHER! BE SURE TO STORE YOUR GRANOLA IN THE FREEZER SO THAT EVERY LITTLE MORSEL STAYS DELICIOUS, NO MATTER HOW HOT YOUR KITCHEN GETS! NO NEED TO THAW IT, JUST POUR THE GRANOLA FROM THE CONTAINER IN THE FREEZER RIGHT INTO YOUR BOWL!

Basic Bar

INGREDIENTS:

Granola Ingredients:

Nuts – almonds, walnuts or peanuts

Old-fashioned oatmeal, dry

Cinnamon

Peanut butter

Pure maple syrup

Raising the Bar

INGREDIENTS:

Additional Granola Ingredient Options:

Combination of nuts – almonds, walnuts, pecans, peanuts, pistachios, cashews

Seeds – sesame seeds, sunflower seeds, pepitas (pumpkin seeds)

Barley flakes or quinoa flakes (not a cold cereal, these look just like uncooked oatmeal)

Almond butter, sunflower seed butter, cashew butter, walnut butter (make in food processor)

Date syrup pg295

Pumpkin Pie Spice pg284

Chai Spice Blend pg282

Ginger, powdered

Unsweetened cocoa/cacao powder

Dried fruit (to add after granola is cooked): apples, raisins, cranberries, blueberries, goji berries, pineapple, peaches

MY OWN ADDITIONS OR IDEAS/RECIPES TO TRY:

_____

_____

_____

_____

FAVORITE INGREDIENTS/COMBINATIONS:

_____

_____

_____

WHO LOVED THIS FOODIE BAR?

_____

SET UP THIS FOODIE BAR AT WHICH SPECIAL EVENTS/PARTIES/POTLUCKS?

_____

NEXT TIME I MAKE THIS FOODIE BAR, I WILL:

_____

_____

*SHOP SMART, PREP SMART, COOK SMART TIPS:

* To make just enough Date Syrup pg295 for this recipe, remove the pits from 4-5 large Medjool dates and combine with ~⅓ cup water and ½ teaspoon vanilla. Soak overnight to soften before blending the mixture until silky smooth (a high-powered blender will do the job with dates that have not been softened/soaked.)
* Parchment paper is a wonderful product to use in baking and dehydrating as nothing sticks and no need for messy pan sprays full of chemicals!

Scot's Granola

My husband and I both LOVE this granola, so does my mom, dad and sister... If I didn't keep it in the freezer, an entire batch might just be gone in a day or so. In fact, it is so well liked, that I make a triple batch every few weeks. Since my oven has 3 racks, I can cook it all at once, on 3 large baking sheets lined with parchment paper. The original recipe used all maple syrup, but Date Syrup pg295 is such a superior choice, since dates taste fantastic and are a whole food, full of fiber and phytonutrients.

INGREDIENTS

½ cup pecans

½ cup walnuts

3 cups of old-fashioned oatmeal, dry

1 Tablespoon ground cinnamon (Ceylon variety)

¼ cup almond butter

~½ cup Date Syrup pg295

1-2 Tablespoons maple syrup, optional

Pinch of salt (optional)

PROCEDURE

1. Make the Date Syrup pg295 in a blender (if you don't already have some).

2. Pre-heat oven to 325-340°F. Line a baking pan with parchment paper.*

3. Pulse the nuts and half of the oats in a food processor.

4. In a large bowl, whisk together the almond butter, cinnamon, date syrup, maple syrup (if using) and pinch of salt until smooth. Stir in the nuts/oat mixture from the food processor and the last 1 ½ cups of oats and mix until very well combined.

5. Spread mixture out into a thin layer on a parchment lined baking sheet and bake at 325-340°F until golden and crunchy, about 30 minutes total – stirring/flipping over the granola with a spatula every 10 minutes or so, to be sure that it cooks evenly. The granola toward the side of the pan tends to darken quicker. Break up any large chunks each time you check on it.

6. Let the granola cool completely before putting it into the freezer in an air-tight storage container. No need to thaw – just use it straight from the freezer.

Recipe adapted by The Nutrition Professor from www.TheVegan8.com

Breakwich Bar

IT IS FUN AND EASY TO EXPERIMENT WITH A VARIETY OF BREADS AND TOPPINGS TO START YOUR MORNING OFF WELL···

Basic Bar

BREAD OPTIONS:

100% Whole Wheat Bread

Whole Wheat English Muffins

Whole Wheat Pita Bread

Whole Wheat Bagel

SPREAD OPTIONS:

Peanut Butter (natural – only ingredients: peanut and maybe, salt)

Strawberry/Raspberry/Blackberry jam (no refined sugar/corn syrup – just fruit)

LAYER ON TOP OF THE SPREAD:

Banana or Apple Slices

Cinnamon

Raising the Bar

BREAD OPTIONS:

Organic 100% Whole Grain Bread Products

Organic Sprouted Whole Grain Bread

Whole Grain Tortilla

Whole Grain Lavash

SPREAD OPTIONS:

Nut Butters: almond butter, walnuts ground into a butter, sunflower seed butter

Nut butter topped with drizzle of Date Syrup pg295

Nut Butter topped with a dessert sauce: T's Dreamy Chocolate Sauce pg286, Dazzle-Berry Sauce pg290, Date Night Caramel Sauce pg288, or Sweet Mango Lime Sauce pg292

Beanutty Spread pg54

Mia's Banana Chocolate Spread pg52
Organic soy or coconut yogurt (thin layer)

LAYER ON TOP OF THE SPREAD:

Fresh Fruit (slices): pear, strawberry, kiwi, peach/nectarine, plum,

And for the very top...

hemp seeds, chia seeds, flax seeds, Chai Spice Blend pg282, pomegranate arils, raspberries, blueberries, blackberries (may roll off)

MY OWN ADDITIONS OR IDEAS/RECIPES TO TRY:

_____

_____

_____

_____

FAVORITE INGREDIENTS/COMBINATIONS:

_____

_____

_____

WHO LOVED THIS FOODIE BAR?

_____

SET UP THIS FOODIE BAR AT WHICH SPECIAL EVENTS/PARTIES/POTLUCKS?

_____

NEXT TIME I MAKE THIS FOODIE BAR, I WILL:

_____

_____

*SHOP SMART, PREP SMART, COOK SMART TIPS:

* When bananas are perfectly ripe, get them into the refrigerator. While the outside skin will brown, the flesh will stay firm for a few extra days.
* Flax seeds are very durable, but once ground, their important fatty acids and phytonutrients are susceptible to destruction, so they need to be kept cold. I buy whole flax seeds, and keep them in the freezer. Then, every 10 days I grind enough to fill a mason jar that I keep in my fridge to have at my fingertips. I use my "flax grinder" (a dedicated a coffee grinder that I bought for under $10).
* Keep all of your nuts and seeds (including delectable walnuts, packed with omega-3 fatty acids) in the freezer. If you have access to a vacuum sealer, seal the nuts/seeds before putting them into the freezer (will extend life well beyond 6-9 months).

Mia's Banana Chocolate Spread

My daughter loves toast, but I don't love anything about the highly processed margarines at the supermarket. One morning, she developed this recipe and I enjoyed it so much that I make a version with flax and walnuts several times a week and eat it with apple slices. Cacao/cocoa powder provides a rich chocolate flavor and is packed with potent phytonutrients, while the banana does a great job adding natural sweetness. When I shared the recipe with my students, several sent me pictures and even video clips to thank my daughter for her creation!

INGREDIENTS

1 ripe banana*

~2 Tablespoons raw cacao or unsweetened cocoa powder (amount based on taste preferences)

¼-½ teaspoon cinnamon

Optional Mix-ins

1 Tablespoons nut or seed butter (almond butter, peanut butter, sunflower seed butter, etc.)

1-2 teaspoons ground flax seeds*

1 Tablespoon walnuts*, crushed

PROCEDURE

1. Mash the banana and incorporate the cacao/cocoa and cinnamon.

2. Stir in any of the optional mix-ins and enjoy on a piece of toasted whole grain bread, topped with banana or apple slices or skip the bread and simply enjoy it as a dip with fresh apple slices.

Beanutty Spread

This recipe quickly became a family favorite! At breakfast, we top a toasted slice of 100% whole grain bread with the spread, then slices of banana and a sprinkle of cinnamon. We also make the kids' lunch sandwiches with the spread, slices of apple or pear, and a sprinkle of cinnamon!

INGREDIENTS

¼ cup natural peanut butter*

1 cup white beans* (cooked from dry or canned and rinsed)

1-2 Tablespoons real maple syrup or Date Syrup pg295

1 teaspoon cinnamon

2-3 teaspoons of water (to thin the spread)

2-3 teaspoons unsweetened cocoa powder (optional – for a hint of chocolate)

PROCEDURE

1. Combine all of the ingredients (except the water) in a food processor until smooth, adding water, 1 teaspoon at a time to achieve the desired thickness.

2. While it can be stored in the refrigerator for a few days, this is a perfect freezer recipe!

3. Transfer to very small storage containers and keep in the freezer. Will last for months! It will be ready to spread once thawed in the fridge overnight.

Recipe adapted by The Nutrition Professor from The Happy Herbivore, by Lindsay S. Nixon.

*SHOP SMART, PREP SMART, COOK SMART TIPS:

* Your peanut butter should only have 1 or 2 ingredients (peanuts and possibly salt).
* You can also substitute any nut butter for the peanut butter: try almond butter, cashew butter or sunflower seed butter.

MEAL BARS

Mediterranean Fajita Bar

Basic Bar

INGREDIENTS:

Corn tortillas

Hummus (store bought)

Variety of Grilled/Roasted Veggies (frozen, challenge can be avoiding oil): Zucchini, Eggplant, Onion, Peppers (thin strips)

Fresh Greens, chopped into chiffonade or confetti-sized pieces

Sun-dried Tomatoes

Olives, Kalamata or Green (stuffed with pimento or garlic)

Roasted Red Peppers (jarred)

Italian Seasoning pg278

Raising the Bar

FAJITA WRAP OPTIONS:

Organic Corn &/or Whole Wheat Tortillas

Homemade Corn Tortillas

SPREAD OPTIONS:

Mediterranean Spread pg260

Go-To Hummus pg148

TOPPING OPTIONS:

Garlic Mushrooms pg234

Quick Mediterranean Roasted Veggies pg216

2-min Broiled Asparagus pg232

Pickled Onions pg238

Artichoke Hearts

Pepperoncinis

Fresh Parsley

Feta Cheeze pg270

Balsamic Vinegar

Creamy Italian Dressing pg116

Baked Sweet Potato Fries pg222

Mia's Garlic Trees pg230

Grilled Eggplant

Grilled Brussels sprouts

Caramelized Onions pg236

Green and Black Olive Tapenade pg262

Power Pesto pg130

MY OWN ADDITIONS OR IDEAS/RECIPES TO TRY:

_____

_____

_____

_____

FAVORITE INGREDIENTS/COMBINATIONS:

_____

_____

_____

WHO LOVED THIS FOODIE BAR?

_____

SET UP THIS FOODIE BAR AT WHICH SPECIAL EVENTS/PARTIES/POTLUCKS?

_____

NEXT TIME I MAKE THIS FOODIE BAR, I WILL:

_____

_____

Greek Fajita

In preparation for a Memorial Day BBQ with our neighbors, I though[t]
to use some delicious grilled veggies and one of my favorite bean sp[read]
fusion dish – Greek Fajitas! Everyone loved it and commented that [they]
thought about putting those flavors together on a tortilla, they were
enjoying that meal again, soon!

INGREDIENTS

Warmed corn tortillas (organic, if possible)

Mediterranean Grilled Veggies pg214: asparagus, sweet potatoes, red onion, zucchini, mushrooms, eggplant and/or red bell pepper

Mediterranean Spread pg260

Toppings:

Kalamata olives, diced small

Fresh parsley, chopped finely

Sun-dried tomatoes, chopped small (rehydrated in water, if dry)

Artichoke hearts, chopped small

Squeeze of fresh lemon juice

PROCEDURE

Grab a warm* tortilla, smooth on a layer of spread, load up the veggies, sprinkle with the toppings, grab a few napkins and enjoy right away!

*SHOP SMART, PREP SMART, COOK SMART TIP:

*   Warm a stack of tortillas wrapped in damp paper towels and then foil, if using BBQ to warm the tortillas while grilling the vegetables. If you are using the microwave to warm the tortillas, wrap in paper towels, but not foil, check after every ~30 seconds.

Burrito Bowl Bar

Basic Bar

INGREDIENTS:

Spinach and crisp lettuce*

Brown Rice (pre-cooked – either frozen or vacuum sealed) or Excellent Brown Rice Every Time pg250

Variety of steamed veggies (fresh or frozen) or grilled/roasted veggies (frozen): zucchini, eggplant, onion, peppers, carrots, green beans, cauliflower

Black beans or chili beans (cooked from dry or canned)

Red Cabbage (thinly slices/shaved)

Scallions, chopped small

Corn (organic frozen)

Olives, sliced

Cilantro

Salsa (store bought)

Avocado

Fresh Lime

---

*SHOP SMART, PREP SMART, COOK SMART TIP:

*   To crisp up romaine, rinse it in cool water, then wrap it in paper towel and put back into fridge in a produce bag.

Raising the Bar

INGREDIENTS:

Mixed salad greens, chopped spinach, or "Power Greens" chopped into chiffonade (ribbons) or confetti-sized pieces

Sofritas pg64 Tofu or Jackfruit

Cilantro Lime Rice pg252

Seasoned Black Beans pg218

Garlic Mushrooms pg234

Grilled Fajita Veggies pg214

2-min Broiled Asparagus pg232

Pickled Onions pg238

Jicama Chips pg242, diced

Corn – fresh from the cob &/or roasted OR Smoky Corn pg240

Beany Guac pg170

Greeny Guac pg172

Fiery Salsa pg176

Homemade salsa (See Salsa Foodie Bar pg174)

Creamy Lime Cilantro Dressing pg118

Cilantro Pesto pg126

Ranch-Style Dressing pg122

Makayla's Fire Roasted Salsa pg178

Baked Sweet Potato Fries pg222

Mia's Garlic Trees

Mexican Quinoa pg248

Cauliflower and Lentil Filling pg220

Grilled Brussels sprouts

MY OWN ADDITIONS OR IDEAS/RECIPES TO TRY:

_____

_____

_____

_____

FAVORITE INGREDIENTS/COMBINATIONS:

_____

_____

_____

WHO LOVED THIS FOODIE BAR?

_____

SET UP THIS FOODIE BAR AT WHICH SPECIAL EVENTS/PARTIES/POTLUCKS?

_____

NEXT TIME I MAKE THIS FOODIE BAR, I WILL:

_____

_____

63

RECIPE USED IN THESE BARS:

Burrito Bowl Foodie Bar
Nacho Foodie Bar

*SHOP SMART, PREP SMART, COOK SMART TIPS:

* To press extra liquid out of water-packed tofu, wrap in paper towels or a clean kitchen towel and top with heavy weights (baking sheet with a few cans on top). Drain for ~30 minutes. Alternatively, you can purchase a tofu press (my favorite: TofuXpress), although a bit pricey, is a great investment if you use it often.
* Do not use silken tofu for this recipe (the type packed in aseptic packaging – a.k.a. juice box)
* When water-packed tofu is frozen (in original container – leave as is and place it directly into the freezer), and then thawed, fluid is easily pressed out and the you'll find that the texture changes, (chewier).
* You can also use 1-2 cloves of fresh garlic, just be sure to press/mince it and let it sit for ~10 minutes before adding it to the hot pan with the onion (to maximize the cancer-fighting power).

Austin's Sofritas Burrito Bowl

I created this recipe as an alternative to going out to Chipotle, as it can get quite expensive to eat out on a regular basis. You can play around with the texture of the tofu based on how you cook it. I tried in a saucepan and in the oven and like the oven version best, as it stayed chewy even after soaking up the delicious sauce. Feel free to make it spicier by leaving in some of the chipotle pepper seeds, adding hot sauce, or more of Austin's Smoky Spicy Blend.

INGREDIENTS

½ cup red onion, diced

4 oz can fire-roasted green chilis

2 teaspoons Austin's Smoky Spicy Blend pg276

2 chipotle peppers in adobo (canned/jarred)* – seeds removed, and finely chopped

2 Tablespoons sun-dried tomatoes (dry, not packed in oil), chopped small

2 Tablespoons tomato paste

6-8 cloves roasted garlic pg228

2 cups low sodium vegetable broth

14-16 oz container of water-packed tofu*

PROCEDURE

1. Preheat oven to 325°F. Crumble the tofu and sprinkle with black pepper and a dash of salt (optional), spread onto baking sheet lined with parchment paper and baked until fairly dry and crunchy (~20-30 minutes).

2. While the tofu is "drying" in the oven, add red onion to a dry saucepan over medium heat, cook until golden and translucent, adding a Tablespoon or two of veggie broth, if needed.

3. Add garlic and cook for 30 seconds, then Austin's Smoky Spicy Blend pg276 and cook for 30 seconds more, stirring constantly to avoid burning, while enhancing flavors.

4. Add the remaining ingredients and simmer until amount has been reduced by ~⅓.

5. When the tofu is "crispy", add to the sauce and turn off heat. The flavors will be even better the next day!

6. Assembling your bowl: Layer the Lime Cilantro Brown Rice pg252, Seasoned Black Beans pg218, Grilled Fajita Veggies pg214, Sofritas, diced cherry tomatoes, red cabbage, avocado and scallions. Add a squeeze of lime!

Pizza Bar

Basic Bar

INGREDIENTS:

Lavash Bread (whole grain)

Jarred Marinara Sauce

Leafy green of your choice, minced finely

Red onions, sliced thin

Olives, sliced thin

Mushrooms, sliced thin

Raising the Bar

SAUCE OPTIONS:

Jarred Marinara Sauce with steamed frozen collard greens and carrot blended in (use blender)

Quick Tomato Sauce pg256

Tomato Almond Pesto pg128

Creamy Pasta Sauce pg258

TOPPING OPTIONS:

Pickled Red Onion pg238

Garlic Mushrooms pg234

Feta Cheeze pg270

Artichoke Hearts

Roasted Butternut Squash

Grilled Eggplant

Vegan grain-based or tofu-based sausage (look for products without "protein isolates" as ingredients)

2-min Broiled Asparagus pg232

Power Pesto pg130

Mia's Garlic Trees pg230

Cheezy Parm pg272

Caramelized Onions pg236

Green and Black Olive Tapenade pg262

Pepperoncinis

CRUST OPTIONS:

Whole Grain Toast

Whole Grain Pita

Grilled Eggplant

Grilled Zucchini

Grilled Portobello

Grilled Polenta

MY OWN ADDITIONS OR IDEAS/RECIPES TO TRY:

_____

_____

_____

_____

FAVORITE INGREDIENTS/COMBINATIONS:

_____

_____

_____

WHO LOVED THIS FOODIE BAR?

_____

SET UP THIS FOODIE BAR AT WHICH SPECIAL EVENTS/PARTIES/POTLUCKS?

_____

NEXT TIME I MAKE THIS FOODIE BAR, I WILL:

_____

_____

*SHOP SMART, PREP SMART, COOK SMART TIPS:

* Any variety of kale can be used for this recipe (green curly kale, lacinato or dinosaur kale and red/purple kale). Rinse the kale under cool running water, rip bite sized pieces of the leaves off of the stems and let them soak in a large bowl of ice water for 5-10 minutes (or up to several hours if you are busy with other tasks). Reserve the stems for later use.* Dry the kale with a salad spinner or by wrapping in paper towel.

* I finely chop the kale stems and add them to our weekly salad mix or mirepoix (carrot, celery and onion) when making soup or I throw them into stir-fries.

Thin Crust Kale Pizza

This delicious recipe is super quick to put together, so it works well for a weeknight dinner or if you are feeding more than just a few, it can be a fun way to get everyone involved in the preparation! You might hesitate when you see kale on the ingredient list, but go ahead and MAKE IT! You will love it and be amazed that you are eating kale! The amounts are approximates, as everyone likes their pizza a little different when it comes to how much of each topping. You may also want to add other toppings, like finely chopped steamed broccoli, very thinly sliced zucchini, garlicky mushrooms, or bell peppers.

INGREDIENTS

~3 cups raw kale (any variety)*, cleaned and finely chopped (confetti-sized pieces)*

~2-4 Tablespoons sun-dried tomatoes, chopped into strips

~4 Tablespoons artichoke hearts, diced small

~2 Tablespoons olives, diced small

~2-4 Tablespoons red onion, sliced thin or Pickled Red Onions pg238

~⅓ cup Quick Tomato Sauce pg256 (or your favorite recipe or brand)

Whole wheat Lavash Bread, large piece ~12 in x 8 in

PROCEDURE

1. Clean and dry the kale (see tips), then chop it finely, to about the size of confetti.

2. Cut the Lavash Bread in half to make 2 "pizzas" and toast in 400°F oven for a few minutes on a pizza screen, until crisp.

3. Spread a layer of sauce on the toasted Lavash bread (must toast without toppings first), then sprinkle on some sun-dried tomatoes, then add a GENEROUS layer of kale (don't be scared!), followed by the chopped olives, artichoke hearts and onions.

4. Put the pizzas back in the oven for 5-8 minutes, just to heat the toppings and begin to wilt the kale.

5. Slice each pizza into six pieces with a chef's knife to make it a bit easier to eat, and start munching as soon as it is cool enough to pick up!

Crazy Salad Bar

Basic Bar

INGREDIENTS:

Mixed Greens

Romaine Lettuce

Beans (canned or cooked from dry)

Broccoli Slaw (sold in produce aisle) (Shredded Red Cabbage, Broccoli and Carrots)

Red onion or Scallions (green onions)

Red, yellow or orange bell peppers, chopped into small pieces

Carrot, grated

Celery, chopped into very small pieces

Apple, chopped in small pieces

Raisins

Pepita (pumpkin) seeds, walnuts or sunflower seeds

Grated fresh beets

DRESSING OPTIONS:

Salad Dressing Foodie Bar - Shaken pg108

Soy Ginger Dressing pg110

Lemon Balsamic Dressing pg112

No oil store bought dressing

Raising the Bar

INGREDIENTS:

Kale, shredded (any variety), spinach, chard, arugula, watercress

Rainbow Salad (Shredded Red Cabbage, Broccoli, Cauliflower and Carrots)

Seasoned Lentils pg246

Roasted Beets with Citrus pg226

Pickled Red Onion pg238

Garlic Mushrooms pg234

Feta Cheeze pg270

Artichoke Hearts

Steamed or roasted sweet potato pg222

Homemade Croutons pg254

Avocado

Tomato

Cucumber

Zucchini

Peas

Goji berries, cranberries

2-min Broiled Asparagus pg232

Mia's Garlic Trees pg230

Cheezy Parm pg272

Edamame, bought already cooked, or boiled for 5 minutes

Radishes

Austin's Marinated Tempeh pg102 or BBQ Tempeh pg104, crumbled

Pepperoncinis

Roasted Red Peppers

DRESSING OPTIONS:

Salad Dressing Foodie Bar - Blended pg114

Creamy Lime Cilantro Dressing pg118

Lemony "Caesar-ish" Dressing pg120

Ranch-Style Dressing pg122

Creamy Italian Dressing pg116

T's Cowboy Salad pg162 + mustard + apple cider vinegar + a few splashes of water (if needed)

MY OWN ADDITIONS OR IDEAS/RECIPES TO TRY:

_____

_____

_____

FAVORITE INGREDIENTS/COMBINATIONS:

_____

_____

_____

WHO LOVED THIS FOODIE BAR?

_____

SET UP THIS FOODIE BAR AT WHICH SPECIAL EVENTS/PARTIES/POTLUCKS?

_____

NEXT TIME I MAKE THIS FOODIE BAR, I WILL:

_____

_____

Timaree's Crazy Salad Base

This salad base has become my staple lunch, as I prepare it on Sunday and divide it up into containers, two for each day (one for me and one for my husband). I add my hearty toppings the night before and pack my dressing separately. I typically rotate through my favorite dressing recipes, to change up the flavors from week to week. I have NEVER grown tired of this salad, I actually look forward to it EVERY DAY! The advanced preparation saves me so much time and money throughout the week, as all I need to do is reach into the fridge, pop the lid open to add dressing, secure the lid, shake it up and grab a fork!

INGREDIENTS

1 bunch of Lacinato kale

1 bunch purple/red kale (remove stems, but keep them to chopped finely)

1 bunch scallions (green onions)

5-9 stalks of celery, with leaves

1 large bunch of parsley

Reserved kale stems

1 pkg Rainbow Salad or Broccoli Slaw (mix of julienned cabbage, carrots, broccoli and cauliflower)

Add hearty toppings to this base (See Crazy Salad Foodie Bar pg70 for a list of toppings to consider).

PROCEDURE

1. Rinse the kale under running water and then add to a large bowl of ice water, to allow any debris to fall away. Then, toss it into a salad spinner (in batches) to remove excess water. The parsley and scallions get the ice water treatment, too, though I am even more thorough when I remove any sand/dirt clinging inside the green stems of the scallions. As these veggies leave the salad spinner, I roll them in paper towel and refrigerate until I am ready to chop and assemble the Crazy Salad Base.

2. I like each bite of my salad to be a great mix of textures and flavors, so I chop all of the delightful vegetables very small. However, before I grab a knife and cutting board, I get out one of my very large catering bowls, so that I have plenty of room to combine all of the ingredients. Then, I finely chop the celery, kale stems, and scallions, adding them to the large bowl. Next, I shred the kale (and then cut across the shredded pieces to end up with medium-sized confetti pieces), and add those to the bowl, along with a bag of "Rainbow Salad" – a sibling of Broccoli Slaw) which contains a mix of julienned purple cabbage, carrots, cauliflower and broccoli.

3. That mixture gets tossed well, and then a one pound container of organic mixed greens, goes in as the last ingredient for the base. I fill a plastic or glass storage container with this salad base for each day (one per person) and store in our garage fridge (temperature stays much more consistent, as the door does not get opened nearly as often as the one on the house). The day or two before I plan to eat each salad, I add the "hearty" toppings (always including a legume) and finish off with a sprinkling of fruit, nuts and/or seeds.

Loaded Potato Bar

Basic Bar

INGREDIENTS:

Baked Potato (with skin)

TOPPING OPTIONS:

Chili beans (look for low sodium varieties, without any animal products)

Greens, fresh or frozen and steamed (chopped small)

Mixed vegetables, steamed

Salsa (store bought)

Hot sauce/Sriracha (if desired)

Lime or lemon (squeeze of juice)

Avocado

Salt/pepper (to taste)

Raising the Bar

INGREDIENTS:

Baked sweet potato with skin (light colored flesh, orange or purple)

TOPPING OPTIONS:

Seasoned Black Beans pg218

Really Quick Sautéed Collard Ribbons pg224

Mia's Garlic Trees pg230

Cheezie Sauce pg266

Garlic Mushrooms pg234

Greeny Guac pg172 or Beany Guac pg170

Olives, chopped/sliced

Colorful bell peppers, chopped small

Homemade salsa pg174

Jalapeño or serrano pepper, diced (seeds and ribs removed unless you like heat)

Red/purple cabbage, shredded

Fresh cilantro, finely chopped

Scallions, finely chopped

T's Cowboy Salad pg162

Austin's Marinated Tempeh pg102 or BBQ Tempeh pg104, crumbled

MY OWN ADDITIONS OR IDEAS/RECIPES TO TRY:

_____

_____

_____

_____

FAVORITE INGREDIENTS/COMBINATIONS:

_____

_____

_____

WHO LOVED THIS FOODIE BAR?

_____

SET UP THIS FOODIE BAR AT WHICH SPECIAL EVENTS/PARTIES/POTLUCKS?

_____

NEXT TIME I MAKE THIS FOODIE BAR, I WILL:

_____

_____

* When choosing sweet potatoes, be sure that they are heavy for their size, firm (no soft spots or wrinkled ends), and of similar size, so that they will roast in about the same time.
* Be sure to roast enough sweet potatoes to use for the rest of the week, so they will be at your fingertips when you come home hungry!
* Any fresh greens will work, including baby spinach, kale or chard.

Southwestern Loaded Sweet Potatoes

This meal is very easy to prepare and super satisfying! Once I explain to my students how to make it, they try it once, and then it becomes a "go-to meal" for busy nights. Tracy (host and producer of *California Bountiful)* and Scott (cameraman extraordinaire) loved it so much, that they stopped on the way home from shooting the TV segment to pick up the ingredients!

INGREDIENTS

Sweet potatoes*, light colored flesh, rinsed, but NOT peeled

Toppings:

Chopped fresh greens*

Beans

Red/Purple cabbage, thinly sliced/shaved

Salsa

Avocado

Cilantro

Scallions, chopped small

Lime (for squeezing)

PROCEDURE

1. Place rinsed sweet potatoes* directly on oven rack (do not wrap in foil) and place a large piece of foil on the rack below to catch any drips. Roast at 350-375°F until tender, approx. 30-40 minutes.

2. Slice steaming hot sweet potato open and fill with chopped greens, then beans (warm up if cold), cabbage, salsa, cilantro, scallions, avocado and a squeeze of lime juice.

Pasta Bar

This bar is a staple at our house, as we set it up for 8 or more dinners each month. We use it for entertaining when we have friends over and even had it at our wedding. We had so many compliments on that meal during the reception, as everyone loved the opportunity to have made-to-order pasta piping hot out of the saute pan!

Basic Bar

NOODLE OPTIONS:

Whole grain pasta* of different shapes and sizes: spaghetti, linguine, penne, rotini, rigatoni

Gluten free pasta: quinoa pasta, brown rice pasta (more options below)

VERY IMPORTANT! Cook pasta VERY al dente (stop cooking it a few minutes earlier than you normally would, because you are going to re-heat it with the sauce)

SAUCE OPTIONS:

Marinara – store-bought

MIX-INS (TO COOK IN PAN BEFORE ADDING COOKED PASTA AND SAUCE):

Red onion, thin slices or very small dice

Sun-dried tomatoes, diced and re-hydrated if dry

Garlic, pressed or finely minced

Fresh greens – chopped kale, spinach, chard, collards or any combination (small confetti sized pieces will be eaten more readily by everyone)

Green or Kalamata olives (cut into quarters and then each quarter into 3-4 pieces)

Mushrooms, sliced

Raising the Bar

NOODLE OPTIONS:

Vegetable noodles: zucchini, carrot, butternut squash, bell peppers, beets (use a standard vegetable peeler, a julienne vegetable peeler or spiralizer to cut vegetables into noodle-shaped pieces),

Shredded cabbage, broccoli slaw/rainbow salad (available packaged in refrigerated section of supermarket produce area).

Black bean pasta, adzuki bean pasta, mung bean pasta, lentil pasta (available in some grocery stores and online)

Shirataki noodles (made from a yam/root and sold in the refrigerated section of the produce aisle – rinse well, boil for 1 minute, then dry the noodles by heating them in a dry pan until they squeak, before adding your choice of sauce).

SAUCE OPTIONS:

Quick Tomato Sauce pg256

Creamy Pasta Sauce pg258 (similar to white Alfredo sauce)

Tomato Almond Pesto pg128

Power Pesto pg130

MIX-IN OPTIONS:

Roasted garlic pg228

Garlic Mushrooms pg234

Asparagus – when in season (bite sized pieces)

Zucchini (small-medium sized pieces – not too big – if small will cook very quickly and get mushy if overcooked, so add once other vegetables are nearly done)

Broccoli (very small florets)

Cauliflower (very small florets)

Artichoke hearts (cut into small pieces)

Tomatoes (fresh, small dice)

Roasted red peppers (do not need to cook, so add at very end)

Grain-based or tofu-based sausage (look for products without "protein isolates" as ingredients)

Mia's Garlic Trees pg230

TOPPING OPTIONS:

Parsley and/or Basil, fresh for top

Toasted whole grain bread crumbs or crushed Homemade Croutons pg254

Cheezy Parm pg272

Brazil Nut Parm pg274

Green and Black Olive Tapenade pg262

MY OWN ADDITIONS OR IDEAS/RECIPES TO TRY:

_____

_____

_____

FAVORITE INGREDIENTS/COMBINATIONS:

_____

_____

_____

WHO LOVED THIS FOODIE BAR?

_____

SET UP THIS FOODIE BAR AT WHICH SPECIAL EVENTS/PARTIES/POTLUCKS?

_____

NEXT TIME I MAKE THIS FOODIE BAR, I WILL:

_____

_____

* Our favorite shapes are penne or rotini, as they mix with the veggies and hold the sauce well, be sure to cook it al dente (under cook by 1-2 minutes), since you will be heating it up with the sauce in the pan.

* Have your favorite pasta sauce waiting for you in the fridge (some of our other favorites are listed in the Pasta Bar section pg78).

* To maximize the amazing power of garlic's phytonutrients, be sure to press it (through a garlic press) or chop it well and let it sit for at least 10 minutes before adding it to the hot pan with the onions and sun-dried tomatoes.

Hagenburger's Party Pasta

We don't wait for a reason to throw a party to make this meal! It is a common dinner at our house, and one of my husband's all-time favorites. A little advanced preparation on the weekends makes this a go-to weeknight meal that rivals any Italian restaurant! (I am Italian and I stand by that proclamation!)

INGREDIENTS

Whole grain penne* pasta, cooked

Tomato Almond Pesto* sauce pg128

Red onion, sliced

Garlic, pressed/minced*

Greens, kale, spinach and/or chard – chopped very small

Asparagus, bite sized pieces (when in season)

Zucchini, bite sized pieces

Grain-based or tofu-based sausage* link, sliced into ½ circle pieces ~¼ inch thick (optional)

Kalamata olives, chopped small

Artichoke hearts (cut into small pieces)

Garlic Mushrooms pg234

Sun-dried Tomatoes

PROCEDURE

1. Cook the onions in a dry saucepan over medium-high heat, until they begin to caramelize. Add a Tablespoon or two of water or veggie broth if they get too dry.

2. Add in the sun-dried tomatoes and garlic, being careful not to burn the garlic.

3. Then add the sausage (if using), asparagus and mushrooms, and cook for a few minutes

4. Add the zucchini and greens cook for 1 minute before adding the pasta, sauce, artichoke hearts and olives. Stir well and "cook" until heated through and greens are just wilted.

Nacho Bar

Basic Bar

INGREDIENTS:

Tortilla chips (organic, if possible)

TOPPING OPTIONS:

Chili beans (look for low sodium varieties, without any animal products)

Salsa (store bought)

Avocado

Hot sauce/Sriracha (if desired)

Lime or lemon (squeeze of juice)

Raising the Bar

INGREDIENTS:

Mia's 1-2-3 Easy Tortilla Chips pg154 (or your favorite from Baked Chip Foodie Bar pg152)

TOPPING OPTIONS:

Cheezie Sauce pg266

Seasoned Black Beans pg218

Mexican Quinoa pg248

Cauliflower Lentil Topping pg220

Austin's Marinated Tempeh pg102, crumbled

Guacamole Foodie Bar pg168

Greeny Guac pg172 or Beany Guac pg170

Black olives, chopped/sliced

Colorful bell peppers, chopped small

Greens, fresh and chopped into very small pieces

Homemade salsa (See Salsa Foodie Bar pg174)

Jalapeño or serrano pepper, diced (seeds and ribs removed unless you like heat)

Tomato, chopped small

Red/purple cabbage, shredded

Scallions, finely chopped

Fresh cilantro, finely chopped

Fiery Fruit Salsa pg176

Makayla's Fire Roasted Salsa pg178

MY OWN ADDITIONS OR IDEAS/RECIPES TO TRY:

_____

_____

_____

_____

FAVORITE INGREDIENTS/COMBINATIONS:

_____

_____

_____

WHO LOVED THIS FOODIE BAR?

_____

SET UP THIS FOODIE BAR AT WHICH SPECIAL EVENTS/PARTIES/POTLUCKS?

_____

NEXT TIME I MAKE THIS FOODIE BAR, I WILL:

_____

_____

Our Favorite Nachos

If given the opportunity, I think that my husband and kids would gladly eat this meal everyday. I make baked chips when I can, but in a pinch, they use store bought organic tortilla chips. We all loved these nachos with Mexican Quinoa and then I made them with the Cauliflower Lentil Topping and we were blown away! You'll have to try both and see which one you like best! Some advanced preparation on the weekend enables us to put this dinner together within a few minutes of arriving home after soccer practice.

INGREDIENTS

Mia's 1-2-3 Easy Tortilla Chips pg154 (or store bought organic tortilla chips)

Cauliflower Lentil Topping pg220 or Mexican Quinoa pg248

Cheezie Sauce pg266 – thinned with water

Scallions, chopped small*

Black olives, chopped small*

PROCEDURE

Arrange the chips on a plate, the add a generous amount of topping, a drizzle of cheezie sauce and sprinkling of scallions and olives.

*SHOP SMART, PREP SMART, COOK SMART TIPS:

* I make up a batch of the Cheezie Sauce p266 and either the Cauliflower Lentil Topping p220 or Mexican Quinoa p248 on the weekend, so that this dinner can come together in a few minutes on busy weeknights.
* Chopping scallions and olives are the perfect jobs for little cooks in training.

Dilla Bar

I cook our dillas in my panini maker, which heats from the top and bottom, so the tortilla gets crispy without having to flip them (as I tend to overfill, which makes flipping quite a challenge). If you are using a traditional saucepan to make your dillas, when you are ready to flip, just cover the dilla with a plate that fits just inside the pan and flip the pan over, holding on to the plate with one hand and the pan with the other. Then, just slide the dilla, uncooked side down, off the plate and into the hot pan.

Basic Bar

INGREDIENTS:

Corn or Whole Grain Flour Tortillas (organic, if possible)

FILLING OPTIONS:

(Choose a theme – Italian, Mexican, Greek…)

Beans (cooked from dry or canned, rinsed and drained WELL)

Hummus (store bought) or pasta sauce (tomato-based, store bought)

Salsa (store bought)

Hot sauce/Sriracha (if desired)

Fresh greens, chopped small

Roasted red pepper (jarred)

Sun-dried tomato

Scallions, chopped small

Broccoli (chopped very small)

Olives, chopped very small

Pineapple, chopped very small

Carrot, finely grated

Tomato, chopped very small

Colorful bell peppers, chopped very small

Jalapeño or serrano pepper, diced (seeds and ribs removed unless you like heat)

Fresh cilantro, finely chopped

Fresh parsley, finely chopped

Avocado (slid inside after it is cooked)

Raising the Bar

INGREDIENTS:

Organic Corn &/or Whole Wheat Tortilla

Homemade corn tortillas

FILLING OPTIONS:

Homemade salsa (Salsa Foodie Bar pg174)

Cheezie Sauce pg266 – a little goes a long way (it can bubble out the sides)

Seasoned Black Beans pg218 – (drain well or the liquid will seep out)

Mexican Quinoa pg248

Cauliflower Lentil Topping pg220

Austin's Marinated Tempeh pg102, crumbled

BBQ Tempeh pg104

Garlic Mushrooms pg234

Really Quick Collard Greens pg224

2-min Broiled Asparagus pg232

Caramelized Onions pg236

TOPPING OPTIONS:

Guacamole Foodie Bar pg168

Greeny Guac pg172 or Beany Guac pg170

Homemade salsa (See Salsa Foodie Bar pg126)

Jalapeño or serrano pepper, diced (seeds and ribs removed unless you like heat)

Tomato, chopped small

Red/purple cabbage, shredded

Scallions, finely chopped

Fresh cilantro, finely chopped

Green and Black Olive Tapenade pg262

Power Pesto pg130

MY OWN ADDITIONS OR IDEAS/RECIPES TO TRY:

_____

_____

_____

FAVORITE INGREDIENTS/COMBINATIONS:

_____

_____

_____

WHO LOVED THIS FOODIE BAR?

_____

SET UP THIS FOODIE BAR AT WHICH SPECIAL EVENTS/PARTIES/POTLUCKS?

_____

NEXT TIME I MAKE THIS FOODIE BAR, I WILL:

_____

_____

Mediterranean Humm-adillas

We invented this family favorite when we had only a few minutes to throw a satisfying meal together and everyone was a bit surprised by how delicious it was!

INGREDIENTS

Timaree's Garlic Mushrooms pg234 (6-7 pieces)

1-2 Tablespoons sun-dried tomatoes, chopped (softened in water if dry)

1 scallion, white and green parts, chopped small

2 large green or Kalamata olives, small dice

2-4 Tablespoons of your favorite hummus (Go-To Hummus pg148)

2 corn tortillas

PROCEDURE

1. Spread the hummus on one side of each of the corn tortillas.
2. Set one tortilla, hummus side up, in a preheated pan. Add the mushrooms, sun-dried tomatoes, scallions and olives so that they are well distributed. Top with other corn tortilla, hummus side down.
3. Cook until bottom tortilla is golden brown, flip and cook until all ingredients are heated through and other tortilla browns, too!
4. Slice into wedges and enjoy, being careful not to burn your mouth on the piping hot filling!

*SHOP SMART, PREP SMART, COOK SMART TIPS:

* If you get in the habit of having all of these ingredients already chopped and ready to go from the fridge to the pan, this yummy meal can be ready in a flash!
* We often use our griddles or have two pans going at once, since everyone loves these!

* By cutting up the toppings small enough, each bite will provide a perfect combination of flavors.
* Even if you are skeptical about the combination of toppings, try it; you just might be pleasantly surprised!
* If you don't have time to make my Quick Tomato Sauce pg256, be sure to have a few jars of sauce in your pantry.

Pizza-dillas

Several years ago, I brought an interactive cooking demonstration to my son's elementary school class. All of the students helped create these "pizza-dillas," made with whole grain tortillas filled with all kinds of produce. As the tortillas browned on the griddle, the kids' excitement grew. As soon as I moved the "pizza-dillas" onto my cutting board, they were vying for their wedge, and as they started eating, I heard, "I can't believe this!" "It is so good!" "Wow, the pineapple gives it just a little sweetness!" "Can we have another slice?" "I didn't think that I'd like all of those vegetables together!" Have fun experimenting with the possibilities!

INGREDIENTS

Whole-grain tortillas

Pizza/Tomato sauce* (Quick Tomato Sauce pg256)

Carrot, finely grated

Spinach, baby variety or chopped very small

Zucchini, chopped very small

Broccoli, chopped very small

Pineapple, chopped very small

Olives, chopped very small

PROCEDURE

1. Spread a few Tablespoons of tomato sauce on half of a whole grain tortilla, then layer with all of the toppings.

2. Cook in a dry pan or griddle until golden brown on each side.

3. Slice into pizza shaped wedges and enjoy as soon as they are cool enough to eat.

Asian Un-Fried Rice Bar

Basic Bar

INGREDIENTS:

Brown Rice, cooked and cooled (bought already cooked – frozen or in vacuum-sealed package, or boil-in-the-bag brown rice – cooked in water or vegetable broth)

Frozen Mixed Vegetables, lightly steamed/microwaved (carrot, corn, peas)

Leafy green of your choice, minced finely (tiny pieces like confetti) (Kale/Spinach/Chard/Collard Greens)

Scallions, chopped small

SEASONING:

Reduced Sodium Soy Sauce + black pepper

GREAT ADDITIONS TO SEASONING:

Garlic + Ginger (fresh is best, but powdered will work) + Sriracha (if you like spicy food)

Raising the Bar

RICE OPTIONS:

Brown Rice, medium grain – cooked in water or veggie broth (Excellent Brown Rice Every Time pg250) and cooled

Red Bhutanese or Black/Purple Rice (same cooking technique as Excellent Brown Rice Every Time pg250) and cooled

COOK-IN/MIX-IN OPTIONS:

Start with…

Red Onion, chopped small – cook in dry pan until beginning to brown, then add in any of these:

Asparagus

Rainbow Salad (Shredded Red Cabbage, Broccoli, Cauliflower and Carrots) – chopped small

Broccoli Florets, bite-sized pieces

Mushrooms, sliced thin

Garlic, pressed/chopped very small

Ginger, grated using a microplane or chopped very small

Tofu, extra firm, water pressed out and crumbled (start in dry, hot pan to brown or add to pan with veggies)

Zucchini, chopped very small — cooks very quickly, cook for only a minute before adding the greens and turning off the heat

Leafy green of your choice, minced finely (tiny pieces like confetti) (Kale/Spinach/Chard/Collard Greens) — added to the pan at the last minute, stir in, put lid on and turn off heat to "wilt" the greens

STIR-IN OPTIONS:

Once all of the Mix-In Options are cooked, add them to the rice and stir in any of these:

Edamame, bought already cooked, or boiled for 5 minutes

Colorful sweet bell peppers, chopped very small

Baby corn, canned

Water chestnuts, rinsed and chopped small

Bamboo shoots, rinsed and chopped small

Scallions, chopped small

Season with "dressing" — 1 Tablespoon reduced sodium soy sauce* + 1 teaspoon rice vinegar + 1 teaspoon sesame seeds + ½ teaspoon miso paste + ¼ teaspoon black pepper + grated ginger

MY OWN ADDITIONS OR IDEAS/RECIPES TO TRY:

_____

_____

_____

FAVORITE INGREDIENTS/COMBINATIONS:

_____

_____

_____

WHO LOVED THIS FOODIE BAR?

_____

SET UP THIS FOODIE BAR AT WHICH SPECIAL EVENTS/PARTIES/POTLUCKS?

_____

NEXT TIME I MAKE THIS FOODIE BAR, I WILL:

_____

_____

*SHOP SMART, PREP SMART, COOK SMART TIPS:

* To enjoy excellent leftover rice for the week, keep the seasoning/dressing separate from the rice until just before serving. Make double the amount listed, keep in a separate container (mason jar works great) and then add it to the warmed rice right before serving, so that the leftover rice doesn't get "soggy".
* You can make your own "reduced sodium soy sauce" by diluting "regular" soy sauce with water – 1:1 ratio – or ½ soy sauce and ½ water.

Weeknight Un-Fried Rice

I like to cook at least 2 cups of medium-grain brown rice on Sunday, so that the kids have it at their fingertips throughout the week. A family favorite is fried rice, but when we go out, we are always disappointed by how much oil is used and how "heavy" we feel afterwards. When I have cooked rice in the fridge, I can whip up this dish in just a few minutes. We can save BIG bucks, everyone feels great when they are done eating and we get delicious leftovers!

INGREDIENTS

6 cups cooked medium-grain brown rice, cooked in veggie broth and cooled*

1 red onion, diced small (can use food processor)

12-16 oz pkg Rainbow Salad (shredded red cabbage, broccoli, cauliflower and carrots) – chopped small (food processor does this quickly)

4-5 cups broccoli florets, bite-sized pieces (can be steamed ahead of time to save time)

2 cloves garlic, pressed/chopped very small

1 inch piece fresh ginger, grated using a microplane or chopped very small

3-4 cups leafy green of your choice, minced finely (tiny pieces like confetti) (kale/spinach/chard/collard greens)

8 oz of edamame, bought already cooked and ready to eat, or boiled for 5 minutes

4 scallions, chopped small (green and white parts)

Seasoning/Dressing*:

~ 2 Tablespoons reduced sodium soy sauce*

1 teaspoon rice vinegar + 1-2 teaspoons sesame seeds

1 teaspoon miso paste + ½ teaspoon black pepper

1 teaspoon grated ginger

PROCEDURE

Cooking Rice:

If you like your rice to be a bit sticky for this recipe, medium-grain or short-grain brown rice is the way to go. Bring 3 ¼ cups of vegetable broth to a boil, stir in 2 cups of rice, put lid on pan and reduce heat until the broth reaches a simmer and leave it alone to cook for ~43-46 minutes (do not lift lid or try to stir it). Once cooked, let the rice "rest" in the pan with the lid on for 5-10 minutes. Spread rice out on a clean baking/cookie sheet to cool quickly. Refrigerate after cooling on cookie/baking sheet for 10 minutes (if not using right away).

Add diced red onion to a dry pan, cooking until it begins to brown, then add the Rainbow Salad (chopped small), garlic and ginger. Add the raw broccoli, (unless already steamed – then add later, as it doesn't need to cook). Once the vegetables are tender crisp, stir in the cooked rice and leafy greens, cover with lid and "wilt" the greens. Stir in the edamame and previously steamed broccoli (if using), scallions and season with reduced sodium soy sauce, or dressing (above) – heat mixture through.

Zuna Bar

GARBANZO BEANS DO QUITE A GOOD JOB FILLING IN FOR TUNA, BUT ARE FREE FROM MERCURY AND CHOLESTEROL, WHILE PROVIDING FIBER, PROTEIN AND A LONG LIST OF IMPORTANT VITAMINS, MINERALS AND PHYTONUTRIENTS.

Basic Bar

INGREDIENTS:

Garbanzo beans (~1 ½ cups cooked from dry or canned and rinsed)
Nori (1-2 sheets chopped into tiny pieces) or ~1 teaspoon dulse

BASIC MIX-INS:

Carrot, grated or chopped into very tiny pieces
Celery, chopped very small
Mayonnaise (Delisa's Mayo pg264)
Relish, pickle
Onion, red, chopped very small
Black pepper, ground
Salt (optional, to taste)

SERVE ZUNA ON:

Romaine lettuce
Zucchini planks
Cucumber rounds
Celery boats/stalks
Whole grain bread
Whole grain crackers

Raising the Bar

INGREDIENTS:

Almonds, chopped
Scallions, white and green parts, chopped small
Shallots, chopped small
Cucumber, diced small or small julienne
Lemons juice and zest
Lime juice and zest
Roasted garlic pg228
Fresh garlic (or granulated garlic powder)
Cumin, ground
Curry powder
Soy sauce
Basil, fresh or dried
Cilantro, fresh
Dill, fresh or dried
Fennel, diced small (in place of celery)
Spinach, chopped small
Parsley, fresh or dried
Thyme, dried
Sun-dried tomatoes
Roasted red peppers
Olives (green and Kalamata are most flavorful)
Capers, with brine (liquid from jar)
Wasabi powder or paste

Miso paste

Avocado

Dijon mustard

Raisins or dried cranberries

Grapes

Jalapeños

Hot sauce

Garlic chili sauce

Ginger

Garlic

Green beans, lightly steamed, cut very small

Asparagus, lightly steamed, cut very small

Radish, water chestnuts &/or jicama,
cut into very small pieces

Fresh red peppers, chopped very small

Beets, raw and finely grated (it will turn your mixture pink!)

Sesame seeds

SERVE ZUNA ON:

Raw red, orange and yellow sweet bell peppers

Jicama Chips pg242

Fennel (cut into sticks like celery)

Radish rounds

Any lettuce (romaine is great)

Cabbage leaves

Kale or chard leaves

Steamed or raw collard green leaf

Seasoned Pita Chips pg156

Baked Chip Foodie Bar pg152

1-2-3 Easy Chips pg154 (seasoned with a sprinkle of salt and pepper)

* Whip up a batch of Delisa's Mayo pg264 in the blender or food processor!
* I am pretty particular with it comes to curry powders, as I like one with a little bit of a natural sweetness to it. Try a few different brands until you find your favorite!
* The nori or dulse are optional, though they are nutrient-dense and in small quantities, provide a hint of "from the sea" flavor.
* It is actually better to err on the side of "not broken up enough" when it comes to the garbanzo beans, so you can smash them with a fork, instead of using the food processor.

Timaree's Curry Zuna

About a decade ago, I tasted a curry tuna sandwich from a catering company in Sacramento (Jealous), and it was so fantastic, that I had to re-create my own version. After going plant-based, it was fun to find that garbanzo beans and a piece or two of nori do a wonderful job replacing the tuna. The ingredients may not seem like they will be good together, but TRUST me. My kids LOVE this recipe!

INGREDIENTS

~3 Tablespoons of Delisa's Mayo pg264 (more to taste, if mixture seems too dry)

2-3 teaspoons curry powder* (or more to taste)

½ teaspoon cinnamon, Ceylon

1 ½ cups garbanzo beans, cooked from dry or canned and rinsed

1-2 pieces of toasted nori (chopped very tiny) OR ~½ – 1 teaspoon dulse flakes (optional)*

1 carrot, grated (small grate)

1 celery stalk, very small dice

1 green onion/scallion, green and white parts, chopped very small

½ cucumber – julienne or diced, small

1 tomato or ~ 1 cup cherry tomatoes, diced small

2 Tablespoons almonds, chopped

½ cup grapes, diced small &/or 2 Tablespoons raisins

PROCEDURE

1. Combine the mayo and spices in a small bowl, set aside.
2. In a food processor with an S-blade in place, pulse the garbanzo beans and finely chopped nori/dulse flakes for just a second at a time, until crumbly – but not a paste (no whole beans left, but still want quite a bit of texture*).
3. Transfer the garbanzo bean mixture to a medium-large bowl and combine with the remainder of ingredients and mix gently, but well. Lastly, stir in the curried mayo.

Spread on… toasted whole grain bread with crispy romaine lettuce, your favorite whole grain crackers, or fresh zucchini planks!

Wrap in… kale or collard leaf (raw or lightly steamed) or a whole grain tortilla/Lavash

Seasoned Tempeh Bar

TEMPEH CAN BE AN ACQUIRED TASTE TO EAT RIGHT OUT OF THE PACKAGE, BUT WITH THE RIGHT MARINADE, YOU MIGHT FIND YOURSELF CRAVING IT BEFORE LONG! SET UP A "TASTE TEST" TO TRY OUT A VARIETY OF DIFFERENT MARINADE OPTIONS WITH A SINGLE PACKAGE OF TEMPEH CUT INTO PLANKS TO DISCOVER YOUR FAVORITES.

Basic Bar

INGREDIENTS:

Organic Tempeh*

MARINADE OPTIONS:

BBQ Sauce (store bought)

Teriyaki Sauce (store bought)

Salsa (store bought)

Buffalo Sauce (store bought)

Raising the Bar

MARINADE OPTIONS:

Austin's Tempeh Marinade pg102

Homemade salsa (See Salsa Foodie Bar pg126)

Reduced-sodium soy sauce + rice vinegar + garlic + ginger

Lime juice + lime zest + garlic + miso + ginger + scallions

Orange juice + zest + garlic + sesame seeds + ginger + oregano

Coconut milk (low fat) + curry powder

Almond milk + Thai curry paste (red, green, yellow or panang)

Add chili garlic sauce, Sriracha or other hot pepper sauce to any of the marinades above for heat!

*SHOP SMART, PREP SMART, COOK SMART TIPS:

* Tempeh is a savory combination of soy beans fermented with a variety of other grains (usually barley, rice and millet) pressed into a "cake" – it is revered as the most beneficial soy product to consume (fermentation increases the nutritional attributes) and provides a wonderful source of plant protein. It is sold in vacuum-sealed packages that freeze perfectly.
* Slice tempeh across short side of cake – into planks (~¼" thick) and marinade for a hour to up to 2 days (in fridge).
* While tempeh can be eaten right out of the package, without any further cooking, it will hold together much better if baked.
* Bake at ~325°F in a single layer, on parchment lined baking sheets, for 15 minutes. Flip each piece and bake for an additional 10 minutes until top of tempeh is no longer "wet" with marinade.
* Store in an air-tight container in the back of the fridge for at least a week.

MY OWN ADDITIONS OR IDEAS/RECIPES TO TRY:

_____

_____

_____

FAVORITE INGREDIENTS/COMBINATIONS:

_____

_____

NEXT TIME I MAKE THIS FOODIE BAR, I WILL:

_____

_____

RECIPE USED IN THESE BARS:

Crazy Salad Foodie Bar
Loaded Potato Foodie Bar
Nacho Foodie Bar
Dilla Foodie Bar

*SHOP SMART, PREP SMART, COOK SMART TIPS:

* You can make your own "reduced sodium soy sauce" by diluting "regular" soy sauce with water – 1:1 ratio – (½ soy sauce and ½ water)
* To maximize the amazing power of garlic's phytonutrients, be sure to press it (through a garlic press) or chop it well and let it sit for at least 10 minutes before adding it to the tempeh marinade, since it contains vinegar and tomato paste (acids).
* Liquid smoke is available at nearly every grocery store and little goes a long way, so you'll only want to add a few drops!

Austin's Marinated Tempeh

This recipe has recently undergone a name change, as my son has taken on the job of preparing a double batch of this tempeh each week. Last summer, when we were talking about lunch options for the upcoming year, both kids told us what they "really wanted" for lunch at school was our tempeh sandwiches. Wow, that was easy! As you can imagine, I was excited! When their peers are eating hot Cheetos and bologna on white bread, my kids are happily chomping down on tempeh (a phenomenal source of protein and incredible phytonutrients), avocado, red onion and romaine lettuce on whole grain bread. Something even more amazing, is that after a year, they didn't grow tired of them and want these sandwiches again this year!

INGREDIENTS

8 oz package of organic tempeh*

Marinade:

2 cloves garlic, pressed/minced*

2 Tablespoons reduced-sodium* soy sauce or tamari

2 Tablespoons vinegar (white, cider, balsamic, rice, red- or white wine)

1 teaspoon ground coriander

½ teaspoon freshly ground black pepper

1 teaspoon date syrup pg295, maple syrup

1 teaspoon Tabasco or other hot sauce

1 Tablespoon tomato paste or ketchup

a few drops of liquid smoke*

1 teaspoon sesame seeds (optional)

PROCEDURE

1. Press/mince garlic and set aside for ~10 minutes, while gathering the rest of the marinade ingredients. Combine the marinade ingredients in a medium size bowl, adding in the garlic and whisk until well mixed.

2. Cut the tempeh into ~20 slices (keep thickness as consistent as possible, for even baking later on), by cutting block in 4 even pieces, then each of those into 5 slices.

3. Place 4-5 tempeh pieces into the marinade, (being careful as they can begin to break apart) and then stack them into a glass baking dish/storage container, repeat with rest of the tempeh, pour any leftover marinade over the tempeh, cover tightly with plastic wrap and refrigerate for at least an hour, or up to 2 days.

4. When you are ready to bake the tempeh, preheat your oven to ~325°F and arrange the tempeh in a single layer, on parchment lined baking sheets. If any marinade remains, re-dip the pieces that were sitting above the liquid, so that they can soak up as much of the marinade as possible, before being baked.

5. Bake at 325°F for 15 minutes, then flip each piece and bake for an additional 10 minutes until top of tempeh is no longer "wet" with marinade. Tempeh will store well in an air-tight container in the back of the fridge throughout the week.

RECIPE USED IN THESE BARS:

Crazy Salad Foodie Bar
Loaded Potato Foodie Bar
Dilla Foodie Bar

BBQ Tempeh

This almost isn't a "recipe" since it is so simple! My son has become our "Tempeh Master" – and he likes making this recipe because he loves BBQ sauce and it is even easier to make than his signature recipe (Austin's Marinated Tempeh pg102). While my kids love to eat this tempeh by itself, we also like it on sandwiches and crumbled into salads (pg70) or as part of our Loaded Potato Bar pg74 (especially on our Southwestern Loaded Sweet Potatoes pg76)!

INGREDIENTS

8 oz pkg tempeh, organic

½ cup BBQ sauce* (store-bought or homemade)

⅓ cup water

2-3 garlic cloves, crushed/minced/pressed*

PROCEDURE

1. Press/mince or chop garlic and let it sit for ~10 minutes.
2. In a large bowl, combine BBQ sauce, water and garlic to make marinade.
3. Slice the tempeh into planks, ~ ¼" thickness, consistent thickness is key for even baking.
4. Dip tempeh slices into marinade and then transfer to a large glass baking dish (9x13), pouring any leftover marinade on top. Marinade in fridge for an hour up to 2 days.
5. When ready to bake, preheat oven at ~325°F and place tempeh in a single layer on parchment paper lined baking sheets.
6. Bake for ~15 minutes, then flip and bake for an additional 10 minutes. Will keep well in tightly sealed container in back of fridge for 1-2 weeks.

*SHOP SMART, PREP SMART, COOK SMART TIPS:

* BBQ sauce – When you choose a BBQ sauce, be sure to check the label to make sure that you avoid high fructose corn syrup, artificial colors/food dyes, caramel color and artificial sweeteners (sucralose, saccharin, etc.). Look for a brand that lists tomato sauce/puree as the first ingredient.
* Garlic tip – To maximize the amazing power of garlic's phytonutrients, be sure to press it (through a garlic press) or chop it well and let it sit for at least 10 minutes before adding it to the marinade.

SAUCE AND DRESSING BARS

Salad Dressing Bar
(Shaken)

I CAN'T REMEMBER THE LAST TIME THAT I BOUGHT A SALAD DRESSING BECAUSE THEY ARE SO EASY TO MAKE, I CAN COMPLETELY CONTROL HOW THEY TASTE, NO CRAZY CHEMICALS AND IT IS WAY CHEAPER! YOU CAN SET UP A SALAD INGREDIENT POTLUCK WITH YOUR BUDDIES (USE THE CRAZY SALAD FOODIE BAR PG70 FOR IDEAS) AND CHALLENGE THEM TO A DIY DRESSING COMPETITION, WITH THE BEST TASTING DRESSING TOSSED WITH A LARGE PORTION OF SALAD AND SERVED TO EVERYONE.

SET UP THIS SALAD DRESSING BAR WHEN YOU DON'T HAVE ACCESS TO A BLENDER. ALL THAT YOU NEED ARE JARS WITH TIGHT FITTING LIDS (CANNING JARS WORK VERY WELL, AS DO PLASTIC SQUEEZE BOTTLES, DEPENDING ON THE SIZE OF THE OPENING AS SOMETIMES HERBS GET STUCK.)

Basic Bar

INGREDIENTS:

1 part fresh squeezed lemon, orange or lime juice

1 part water or vegetable broth, as is, or thickened (whisk in 1 teaspoon arrowroot or corn starch, bring to a boil, then chill in fridge)

1 part vinegar of your choice (natural rice vinegar, apple cider vinegar, coconut vinegar, red wine vinegar, white wine vinegar, balsamic vinegar)

1-2 teaspoons chia seeds (optional)

FLAVOR BOOSTERS:

Mustard (spicy brown)

Granulated garlic powder, onion powder, powdered ginger

Dried Herbs/Spices – oregano, basil, parsley, chives, dill, marjoram, rosemary, tarragon, turmeric, black pepper, white pepper, Italian Seasonings pg278

Raising the Bar

FLAVOR BOOSTERS:

Specialty flavored vinegars

Mustard – stone-ground or Dijon

Garlic – fresh (minced/pressed – be aware that the flavor will get stronger with time) or roasted garlic pg228 (sweet, mild flavor)

Ginger, fresh (use microplane to grate)

Scallions, chopped

Citrus zest – lemon, orange, lime, tangerine

Date syrup pg295, date sugar or maple syrup (based on taste preference)

MY OWN ADDITIONS OR IDEAS/RECIPES TO TRY:

_____

_____

_____

_____

_____

FAVORITE INGREDIENTS/COMBINATIONS:

_____

_____

_____

_____

_____

NEXT TIME I MAKE THIS FOODIE BAR, I WILL:

_____

_____

*SHOP SMART, PREP SMART, COOK SMART TIPS:

* Make a salad base from your favorite chopped greens, shredded cabbage, carrots, broccoli, red pepper and scallions. For a Tex-Mex spin, add cilantro, jicama, black beans, corn and avocado. Or, for an Asian spin, add mint, snow peas, edamame, water chestnuts and avocado!
* Always zest your citrus before cutting to squeeze for juice. A microplane works wonders for zesting, as well as for grating ginger. Be sure to only scrape off the very top layer of the ginger (or not peel it at all), as many of the healthful nutrients are just underneath the skin.

Soy Ginger Lime Dressing

This dressing is light and spunky! All that you need is a glass jar to shake it in! Your microplane will come in very handy to zest the citrus and grate the fresh ginger (if using). Enjoy this dressing on a crispy salad* with a Tex-Mex feel or Asian flair! This makes a little more than ½ of a cup, so you will probably want to double or triple the recipe!

INGREDIENTS

2 Tablespoons freshly squeezed orange juice* & zest (~1 ½ cuties/mandarins)

2 Tablespoons fresh lime juice* & zest (~1 lime)

1 Tablespoon rice wine vinegar (labeled as natural – no added salt or sugar)

1 Tablespoon maple syrup (or Date Syrup pg295)

1 Tablespoon reduced sodium soy sauce

¼ teaspoons crushed red pepper flakes (more or less – to taste)

1 Tablespoon freshly grated* ginger (or ½ teaspoon ground ginger for the Tex-Mex version described in Tips)

PROCEDURE

1. Zest the orange/cuties and lime, then squeeze for the juice.

2. Combine all ingredients in a glass jar (a small mason-type jar works great).

3. Shake and use on your favorite combination of delectable fruits and veggies!

4. Leftover dressing can be refrigerated for at least a week, though it will likely be gone in no time!

Dressing Recipe adapted from http://www.straightupfood.com

RECIPE USED IN THESE BARS:

Crazy Salad Foodie Bar

*SHOP SMART, PREP SMART, COOK SMART TIPS:

* Meyer lemons are phenomenal in this dressing! A friend of mine has a tree and I get so excited when she delivers a bag of lemons before our morning run!
* You can double or triple the recipe since it will last in the refrigerator for several weeks. Just give the jar a shake and toss with your favorite salad mix!
* If you have access to fresh oregano, double the amount (1 teaspoon).
* If you love garlic, you can use 1-2 cloves of fresh garlic, but be sure to mince/crush and let it rest for at least 10 minutes before adding to the dressing (let the cancer-fighting compounds form before combining with vinegar/lemon juice).

Lemon Balsamic Dressing

This dressing is extremely simple and comes together in just a few minutes – no blender needed, just a jar to shake.

INGREDIENTS

⅓ cup lemon* juice

lemon zest 1-2 teaspoons

⅓ cup balsamic vinegar*

⅓ cup water

½ teaspoon oregano, dried*

½ teaspoon granulated garlic powder*

a dash (1/16 teaspoon) turmeric

¼ teaspoon black pepper, ground

1 teaspoon chia seeds

PROCEDURE

1. Combine all ingredients in a clean glass jar and shake until well combined.
2. Will keep in the fridge for at least 2 weeks.

Salad Dressing Bar
(Blended)

A BLENDER (ESPECIALLY A HIGH-POWERED ONE) IS AN AMAZING, TRANSFORMATIVE TOOL WHEN IT COMES TO MAKING CREAMY SALAD DRESSINGS. THE POSSIBILITIES ARE LITERALLY ENDLESS! HAVE LOTS OF SQUEEZE BOTTLES READY TO FILL, AND HAVE FUN EXPERIMENTING. YOU MAY NEVER BUY ANOTHER JARRED DRESSING AGAIN!

Basic Bar

INGREDIENTS:

1 part – fresh squeezed lemon, orange or lime juice

1 part – water or vegetable broth, as is, or thickened (whisk in 1 teaspoon arrowroot or corn starch, bring to a boil, then chill in fridge)

1 part – vinegar of your choice (natural rice vinegar, apple cider vinegar, coconut vinegar, red wine vinegar, white wine vinegar, balsamic vinegar)

1-2 teaspoons chia seeds (optional)

GET CREAMY:

1-3 Tablespoons soaked nuts/seeds (raw sunflower seeds, cashews, almonds, walnuts, pecans, peanuts)

2-4 Tablespoons beans (cooked from dry or canned and rinsed)

3-6 oz silken tofu

½ cup mango, papaya, avocado, zucchini, pears, berries

FLAVOR BOOSTERS:

Mustard (spicy brown)

Granulated garlic powder, onion powder, powdered ginger

Dried Herbs/Spices – oregano, basil, parsley, chives, dill, marjoram, rosemary, tarragon, turmeric, black pepper, white pepper, Italian Seasonings pg278

Raising the Bar

FLAVOR BOOSTERS:

Specialty flavored vinegars

Mustard – stone-ground or Dijon

Garlic – fresh (minced/pressed – be aware that the flavor will get stronger with time) or roasted garlic pg228 (sweet, mild flavor)

Ginger, fresh (use microplane to grate)

Scallions, leeks, red onion, chopped

Citrus zest – lemon, orange, lime, tangerine

Sun-dried tomatoes

Soaked dates, dried plums, raisins, Date Syrup pg295

Apples, peaches, grapes, pomegranate arils, cucumber, tomato, bell pepper (fresh or roasted)

Fresh Herbs: parsley, dill, basil, cilantro, chives, oregano, tarragon

Seeds: Chia seeds, flax seeds, hemp seeds, pumpkin seeds (pepitas), sesame seeds

Be sure to keep track of your TASTY combinations!

MY OWN ADDITIONS OR IDEAS/RECIPES TO TRY:

_____

_____

_____

_____

_____

FAVORITE INGREDIENTS/COMBINATIONS:

_____

_____

_____

_____

_____

_____

NEXT TIME I MAKE THIS FOODIE BAR, I WILL:

_____

_____

*SHOP SMART, PREP SMART, COOK SMART TIPS:

* If you double the recipe, it will keep in the fridge all week. Simply shake well and enjoy!
* Unless otherwise noted, when a recipe calls for a scallions/green onions, use both the white and green parts.
* Fresh herbs (basil and oregano) can be used in place of the dried herb, but the amount should be doubled.

RECIPE USED IN THESE BARS:

Crazy Salad Foodie Bar

Mediterranean Fajita Foodie Bar

Creamy Italian Dressing

This dressing is so creamy, that you will never believe it is the artichokes that do it! It was published in *California Bountiful Magazine* as part of a piece they did on me about my Market Watch segments on their weekly television program.

INGREDIENTS

⅓ cup red wine vinegar

2 scallions/green onions*

⅓ cup water

½ teaspoons dried basil*

½ teaspoons dried oregano*

1 date, pitted (or 1 teaspoon maple syrup)

4 marinated artichoke hearts (~ 8 quarter pieces)

1 garlic clove, pressed/minced

2 teaspoon mustard, spicy brown or Dijon

1 Tablespoon nutritional yeast (optional)

PROCEDURE

Combine all ingredients except the pepper in a blender or food processor. Puree until smooth. Add freshly ground pepper to taste.

Creamy Lime Cilantro Dressing

This dressing packs a ton of flavor for a fraction of the calories in traditional dressing! (26 kcals per ¼ cup vs ~400 kcals!) No one will ever know that this recipe gets its creaminess from tofu. Use half of a box for this dressing and the other half in a Wildly Delicious Strawberry Smoothie pg188.

INGREDIENTS

¼ cup fresh cilantro

½ teaspoons ginger, peeled* & chopped

1 garlic clove, chopped

2 green onions, chopped

2 limes, use zest* and juice

2 teaspoons white wine vinegar

¼ teaspoons salt

2 teaspoons softened raisins (or 1 teaspoon Date Syrup pg295 or maple syrup)

1 Tablespoon Dijon mustard

6 oz silken tofu (½ "box")

PROCEDURE

Combine all ingredients in blender and blend until smooth.

*SHOP SMART, PREP SMART, COOK SMART TIPS:

* Just barely peel ginger, using the back of a spoon (not a vegetable peeler), as many of the powerful antioxidants reside just below the skin!
* Be sure to zest lime (with a microplane, if you have one) before squeezing it for the juice.

RECIPE USED IN THESE BARS:

Crazy Salad Foodie Bar

**Mediterranean Fajita
Foodie Bar**

*SHOP SMART, PREP SMART, COOK SMART TIPS:

* Soaking the cashews is not mandatory, but if you don't have a high-powered blender, the pre-soak will help you to achieve a very creamy texture. If soaking overnight, store in refrigerator.
* Lemon zest, shown to be a potent skin cancer fighter, is easily obtained with a microplane, before cutting a lemon to squeeze it.
* To maximize the health benefits of garlic, chop/press it and let it rest for 5-10 minutes before putting it in contact with acidic foods/liquids or heat.

Lemony "Caesar-ish" Salad Dressing

This dressing has hints of Caesar-flavors and is absolutely delicious! Enjoy it on a mixture of crisp greens, and crunchy julienned veggies (carrot, broccoli, cauliflower and red cabbage), add ripe tomatoes and Homemade Croutons pg254, baked garbanzo beans &/or dried fruit. I also love the addition of grated raw zucchini, diced cucumber and scallions.

INGREDIENTS

½ cup water

1 Tablespoons cashews, soaked* in water

2 Tablespoons white beans, cooked from dry or canned and rinsed

2 Tablespoons lemon juice (fresh squeezed is best* – zest first)

2 Tablespoons Dijon or spicy brown mustard

1 Tablespoon capers with brine (water in jar)

~1 Tablespoon raisins

1-2 cloves garlic, pressed or chopped*

1 teaspoon dried Italian Seasoning (store-bought or pg278)

2 teaspoons chia seeds

Black pepper to taste

PROCEDURE

Combine all ingredients in a high speed blender until very creamy. Will keep well in a tightly-sealed glass jar in the refrigerator at least a week. I like to double the recipe!

Recipe adapted by The Nutrition Professor from www.straightupfood.com by Cathy Fisher

RECIPE USED IN THESE BARS:

Burrito Bowl Foodie Bar
Crazy Salad Foodie Bar

*SHOP SMART, PREP SMART, COOK SMART TIPS:

* If you love lemon and would like a "lemony ranch", be sure to zest the lemon first with a microplane, and then squeeze for juice.
* For a smoky or spicy spin, add a canned or jarred chipotle pepper (remove seeds) or a roasted red bell pepper!

Ranch Style Dressing

This dressing is amazingly creamy, even though it doesn't have any oil or mayonnaise! Play around with the spices and herbs to suit your taste preferences. If you like garlic, add some Roasted Garlic pg228 or fresh if you like a little "bite"… You can also add a chipotle pepper for some major heat and smokiness (canned chipotle in adobo, with seeds removed, unless you really like it very spicy)!

INGREDIENTS

3 Tablespoons raw sunflower seeds (out of the shell), soaked in water ~30 mins to overnight (in fridge)*

3 Tablespoons white beans, cooked from dry or canned and rinsed

2-3 Tablespoons lemon juice*

4 Tablespoons water

2 teaspoons soft raisins (or 1 teaspoon maple syrup)

1 ½ teaspoons cider vinegar

½-1 teaspoon garlic granules (or 2 cloves roasted garlic)

½ teaspoons onion powder

¼-½ teaspoons dried dill

¼-½ teaspoons mustard powder

2 Tablespoons fresh parsley (or 2 teaspoons dried)

¼-½ teaspoons black pepper (more or less – to taste)

Pinch of salt (more or less – to taste)

PROCEDURE

Soak the sunflower seeds in water for at least 30 minutes, up to 24 hours (in fridge). Rinse the seeds and add them to the blender, along with the rest of the ingredients. Blend until smooth and creamy! The dressing will thicken once it is cooled in the refrigerator. Enjoy as a dressing on your favorite salad or as a dip for crunchy veggies! If you end up with any leftover dressing, it will stay good in the fridge for several days to a week.

Recipe adapted from http://www.plantplate.com

Pesto Bar

TIME TO HAVE YOURSELF A PESTO PARTY! ENJOY PESTO ON PIZZA, PASTA, SPIRALIZED VEGETABLE NOODLES (ZUCCHINI, CARROT, BUTTERNUT SQUASH, BEETS), CRACKERS, AS A DIP FOR RAW OR LIGHTLY STEAMED VEGGIES, OR AS AN INGREDIENT IN OTHER RECIPES LIKE LASAGNA OR POLENTA.

Basic Bar

INGREDIENTS:

Fresh basil

Fresh garlic

Lemon juice

Walnuts or pine nuts

Beans, cooked from dry (or canned and rinsed)

Vegetable broth

Salt/pepper to taste

Raising the Bar

INGREDIENTS:

Tomatoes, fresh and/or sun-dried

Fresh herbs: parsley, cilantro, mint

Fresh greens: kale, spinach, chard, collard greens

Nuts/Seeds (soaked in water overnight): almonds, cashews, sesame seeds, chia seeds

Pepperoncinis, jalapeños

Roasted red peppers

Olives, black, green or Kalamata

Roasted Garlic pg228

Miso paste (see tip on pg130)

Italian Seasoning pg278

Zucchini

Green and Black Olive Tapenade pg262

MAJOR BONUSES - YOU SCORED!

* Turn your pesto into a salad dressing! Just add spicy brown mustard, a few Tablespoons of your favorite vinegar and water or vegetable broth (a very small amount at a time) to your pesto to reach the thickness that you like. If the flavor is too strong, add some extra cooked beans and/or mild flavored nut like cashews or almonds soaked (in water to soften), thinning out with water or vegetable broth, if too thick.
* Pesto freezes! Just keep the amount that you'll use over the next few days in the fridge and freeze the rest in small containers – with plastic wrap covering the surface, before popping the lids on, to limit exposure to oxygen. Freeze pesto in ice cube trays, once solid, pop them out and store in a zip-top freezer bag.

MY OWN ADDITIONS OR IDEAS/RECIPES TO TRY:

_____

_____

_____

FAVORITE INGREDIENTS/COMBINATIONS:

_____

_____

WHO LOVED THIS FOODIE BAR?

_____

SET UP THIS FOODIE BAR AT WHICH SPECIAL EVENTS/PARTIES/POTLUCKS?

_____

NEXT TIME I MAKE THIS FOODIE BAR, I WILL:

_____

_____

RECIPE USED IN THESE BARS:

Burrito Bowl Foodie Bar
Pizza Foodie Bar
Nacho Foodie Bar
Dilla Foodie Bar

Cilantro Pesto

I like to keep this bold flavored pesto in a squeeze bottle so that I can drizzle some on my nachos, grilled veggie kabobs, rice and beans or in a wrap. I also like to add equal parts of apple cider vinegar and water, along with a spoon of spicy brown mustard to make a yummy salad dressing that really goes well with fresh tomatoes.

INGREDIENTS

1 cup fresh cilantro, rinsed (bathed in ice water)

¼ cup parsley or basil (optional)

¼ cup cooked white beans

1 Tablespoon walnuts

1 cup raw zucchini

2 cloves garlic*

2 Tablespooons lime juice

3 green olives*

PROCEDURE

Combine all ingredients in a high-powered blender and blend until creamy. Store in an airtight container in the back of the refrigerator for up to 3 days.

*SHOP SMART, PREP SMART, COOK SMART TIPS:

* To maximize the amazing power of garlic's phytonutrients, be sure to press it (through a garlic press) or chop it well and let it sit for at least 10 minutes before adding it to the pesto ingredients, since it contains lime juice.
* While most pesto recipes include quite a bit of oil, this pesto utilizes whole food sources of fat instead, most notably walnuts and olives. Did you know that ~44 olives need to be pressed to make each Tablespoon of olive oil? I'll take the olives, thank you!

Tomato Almond Pesto

On several occasions, I have heard my husband say that if he was ever stuck on a deserted island and could only have one meal, pasta with this sauce would be it… And he isn't even the Italian one in the family! I typically double this recipe and it will stay good for more than a week if I divide it up into 2 containers, and put one towards back of the garage refrigerator, since it rarely gets opened throughout the day and stays much colder!

INGREDIENTS

¼ cup almonds, raw or lightly toasted (soaked in water for a few hours or overnight in the fridge)

12 oz cherry tomatoes*

½ cup fresh basil

1 garlic clove, pressed/minced*

½-1 teaspoon salt (optional)

1-2 pepperoncini* or banana pepper (sold in jars)

¾ cup cooked dark colored beans (cooked from dry or ½ can, rinsed)

PROCEDURE

1. Combine all ingredients in a food processor (or high speed blender) and process until very smooth.
2. Add water or vegetable broth if too thick.
3. Enjoy on whole grain pasta or vegetables noodles, with a variety of grilled/sautéed/roasted veggies!

*SHOP SMART, PREP SMART, COOK SMART TIPS:

* 12 ounces of cherry tomatoes is equivalent to approximately 2 ½ cups.
* To maximize the amazing power of garlic's phytonutrients, be sure to press it (through a garlic press) or chop it well and let it sit for at least 10 minutes before adding heat or acid (e.g. tomatoes in this recipe).
* Only use a clean utensil to remove the pepperoncinis from the jar and you will find that a jar will keep in the refrigerator for months!

SHOP SMART • COOK SMART
EAT SMART

RECIPE USED IN THESE BARS:

**Mediterranean Fajita
Foodie Bar**

Pizza Foodie Bar

Pasta Foodie Bar

Dilla Foodie Bar

Power Pesto

This is not your ordinary pesto, it is actually quite extraordinary!!! In just a few minutes, you'll have a delicious sauce that combines simple ingredients that are some of the highest achievers when it comes to feeling great from the inside out! Use it on pasta, pizza, in lasagna or stuffed mushrooms, or as a dip for lightly steamed veggies or whole grain crackers.

INGREDIENTS

5 oz of "power greens" (any combination of kale, chard, spinach)

¼ cup fresh basil

¼ cup fresh parsley

2 Tablespoons walnuts

2 scallions, chopped

1-2 Tablespoons miso paste*

1 Tablespoon lemon juice

¼ cup beans, cooked from dry or canned and rinsed

5 cloves Roasted Garlic pg228 (if using fresh garlic see tip* below)

PROCEDURE

Combine all ingredients in a food processor and pulse until well mixed, then puree until desired texture is achieved.

Recipe inspired by Nava Atlas' Spinach Miso Pesto in Vegan Express.

*SHOP SMART, PREP SMART, COOK SMART TIPS:

* Miso is a fermented product (think yummy miso soup), most commonly available in the refrigerated section of the produce area in the grocery store. Many products use soybeans and rice or barley, but there are also some alternatives if you are allergic to soy, including chickpea miso (some brands are also gluten-free). It will last in the fridge for months.
* If you decided to use fresh garlic instead – start with 1 clove, as the flavor is much stronger and will only intensify with time.

SNACK BARS

Banana Bread Snack Cake Bar

THIS IS AN EASY RECIPE TO MAKE ON YOUR OWN, BUT IS ALSO FUN WITH SOME FRIENDS IN A BAR SET UP SO THAT YOU CAN TRY DIFFERENT COMBINATIONS. IF YOU ARE MAKING MORE THAN ONE CAKE/LOAF, AND HAVE A GOOD SIZE OVEN, YOU CAN BAKE THEM TOGETHER, BUT HAVE EVERYONE MAKING UP THEIR OWN BATTER AT THE SAME TIME. HAVE THE PARCHMENT PAPER LINED BAKING DISHES READY, SINCE YOU WANT TO GET THE BATTER IN THE OVEN AS QUICKLY AS POSSIBLE AFTER MIXING THE WET AND DRY INGREDIENTS.

Basic Bar

INGREDIENTS:

For each "cake" – use a 7 x 10 baking dish (or equiv)

3 medium to large ripe bananas

2 Tablespoon nut butter*

1 teaspoon vanilla

½ teaspoon salt

¾ teaspoon baking soda

¾ cup coconut sugar*

½ teaspoon spice or blend *

½ cup chopped nuts*

2 cups whole grain flour* (or combination of two)

Raising the Bar

INGREDIENTS:

Nut Butter Options: peanut butter (chunky or creamy – only ingredients: peanuts & maybe salt), almond butter, sunflower seed butter, cashew butter, walnut butter

Sweetener Options: date sugar, coconut sugar

Spice Options: cinnamon, Pumpkin Pie Spice pg284, Chai Spice Blend pg282

Nut Options: pecans, walnuts, almonds, pistachios, peanuts

Whole Grain Flour Options: buckwheat flour, barley flour, kamut flour, whole wheat pastry flour, whole wheat flour, oat flour, spelt flour, quinoa flour

PROCEDURE: (HOW TO DO IT!)

1. Line a 7x10 glass baking pan with parchment paper and set aside. Preheat oven to 350°F.

2. In a large bowl, mash the bananas with a fork, (a large serving fork works well). Add the nut butter, vanilla, salt, baking soda, coconut/date sugar, cinnamon/spice blend and chopped nuts. Add the flour(s) and stir to combine. Note: The batter will be very thick, don't add more liquid or over-mix, it will come out fine!

3. Add the batter to the parchment paper lined baking dish, spreading it out to reach the edges of the pan.

4. Bake at 350°F for ~35 minutes or until toothpick inserted in center emerges clean.

MY OWN ADDITIONS OR IDEAS/RECIPES TO TRY:

_____

_____

_____

FAVORITE INGREDIENTS/COMBINATIONS:

_____

_____

_____

WHO LOVED THIS FOODIE BAR?

_____

SET UP THIS FOODIE BAR AT WHICH SPECIAL EVENTS/PARTIES/POTLUCKS?

_____

NEXT TIME I MAKE THIS FOODIE BAR, I WILL:

_____

_____

* Don't throw away another banana that over ripened! Keep a stash of peeled ripe bananas in the freezer for recipes like this one, smoothies or homemade ice cream!
* If someone in the family is allergic to peanuts, substitute almond butter or sunflower seed butter.
* To make this recipe gluten free, simply experiment with different combinations of gluten-free flours.
* For a chai flavor, instead of the cinnamon, add ½ teaspoon of my Chai Spice Blend recipe pg282.

Banana Pecan Snack Cake

This is a recipe that my kids have been requesting on weekly basis. The ingredient list is short, so it comes together in just a few minutes and produces a fairly dense, yet very satisfying snack cake that I cut into small squares and keep in a plastic container in the fridge. I have had to divide up the pieces into two container and put one the garage fridge, so it can last more than a few days. Otherwise, my family will eat it all in a flash! We have all enjoyed the earthy flavor that buckwheat flour imparts. Bonus: no oil, as a nut butter provides some fat. Double Bonus: Kids can help make it and taste the batter because the recipe doesn't use eggs! See tips for gluten-free/peanut-free options.

INGREDIENTS

3 medium to large ripe bananas* (or 4 smaller bananas)

2 Tablespoons peanut butter*

1 teaspoon vanilla

½ teaspoon salt

¾ teaspoon baking soda

¾ cup coconut sugar

½ teaspoon cinnamon*

½ cup chopped pecans

2 cups of whole grain flour* (I like a mixture of 1 cup buckwheat flour and 1 cup kamut or barley flour – you can also use whole wheat pastry flour.)

PROCEDURE

1. In a large bowl, mash the bananas with a fork, (a large serving fork works well). Add the peanut butter, vanilla, salt, baking soda, coconut sugar, cinnamon and chopped pecans. Add the flour and stir to combine. Note: The batter will be very thick, don't add more liquid, just proceed!

2. Line a 7x10 glass baking pan with parchment paper and add the batter, spreading it out to reach the edges of the pan.

3. Bake at 350 degrees for ~35 minutes or until toothpick inserted into center emerges clean.

Recipe adapted by The Nutrition Professor from the Alternative Vegan, by Dino Sarma.

Kale Chips Bar

LINE UP YOUR BAKING SHEETS AND HAVE A KALE CHIP CHALLENGE!

Basic Bar

INGREDIENTS:

Kale, cleaned* and ripped into bite size pieces – any variety!

Experiment with curly kale – red/purple or green, lacinato or dinosaur kale and baby kale *(Make note of how the type of kale impacts the flavor of the finished product!)*

LIQUID OPTIONS:

To season and/or help other ingredients stick:

Water

Coconut aminos

Soy sauce (reduced-sodium), gluten-free tamari, vegetable broth

DRY INGREDIENTS:

Granulated garlic powder

Sesame seeds

Salt (if not using soy sauce/tamari)

Raising the Bar

INGREDIENTS:

(Make a paste with a fork or food processor, with a variety of ingredients that might go well together to massage on kale pieces – taste your concoction with a toothpick before putting it on the kale):

Citrus zest* and juices: orange, lemon, lime, tangerine/Mandarin

Date sugar/syrup pg295 or maple syrup

Liquid smoke (a few drops go a long way)

Cooked beans or lentils (~1-2 Tablespoons per batch – pureed)

Nut butters: peanut, almond, cashew, walnut

Sun-dried tomatoes (re-hydrated in water, if dry and chopped very small or pureed)

Nutritional Yeast (flakes) – for a hint of cheesy flavor

Cayenne, Sriracha, chili garlic sauce, hot sauce

Roasted Garlic pg228

Italian Seasoning pg278, curry powder, Austin's Smoky Spicy Blend pg276, smoked paprika, cumin, coriander, Cheezy Parm pg272

See my Back to Basics Kale Chips recipe pg140 for details about how to clean/prep the kale and avoid burning the chips!

MY OWN ADDITIONS OR IDEAS/RECIPES TO TRY:

_____

_____

_____

_____

FAVORITE INGREDIENTS/COMBINATIONS:

_____

_____

_____

WHO LOVED THIS FOODIE BAR?

_____

SET UP THIS FOODIE BAR AT WHICH SPECIAL EVENTS/PARTIES/POTLUCKS?

_____

NEXT TIME I MAKE THIS FOODIE BAR, I WILL:

_____

_____

*SHOP SMART, PREP SMART, COOK SMART TIPS:

* I chop the kale stems into tiny pieces to use in my weekly salad mix or in a stir-fry.
* Make your own reduced-sodium soy sauce by diluting 1 part regular soy sauce with 1 part water (2 teaspoons of each for this recipe)
* Parchment paper is a wonderful product to use in baking and dehydrating as nothing sticks and no need for messy pan sprays full of chemicals!
* I love my salad spinner, which I bought for less than ~$20. I use it for my weekly salad mix and any-time I am making kale chips or prepping fresh herbs (cilantro, parsley, basil, etc.). If you don't have a salad spinner, as you remove your clean greens from their ice water bath, just give them a shake over the sink and then wrap in paper towel to remove excess water.

Back to Basics Kale Chips

Although I tend to enjoy a variety of flavors on my kale chips, my son and husband love this very basic version. It seems almost too simple for a recipe, but it just might be the perfect starting place for you! The secret to kale chips is cooking them at low heat until crispy. Although many recipes out there recommend temperatures above 400°F, that has never resulted in anything but burnt, bitter kale that I have to throw away. You can also make these kale chips in a dehydrator, if you have one (~110°F for ~8 hours).

INGREDIENTS

1 bunch kale, red/purple or green, organic (if possible)

4 teaspoons coconut aminos, reduced-sodium* soy sauce, or gluten-free tamari (based on flavor preference)

Parchment paper* (for baking sheet)

PROCEDURE

1. Pre-heat oven to 280°F. Line a baking pan with parchment paper.

2. Rinse the kale under running water, being sure to remove any dirt along the stem. Remove the kale from the stem* by tearing off bite sized pieces and adding them to a large bowl of ice water, to allow any extra debris to fall away.

3. Toss the kale into a salad spinner* (in batches) to remove excess water and then into a clean produce bag.

4. Add the coconut aminos or soy sauce to the kale in the bag, hold the bag closed and shake it up!!!

5. Once the kale is well coated, place kale pieces on a parchment paper lined baking sheet, trying not to overlap. You may end up with multiple pans of kale chips, depending on the original size of the kale bunch.

6. Bake at ~280°F (convection, if possible) until crispy, ~6-20 minutes, depending on oven and thickness of kale leaves. Test them for crispiness frequently, as you do not want them to burn.

*SHOP SMART, PREP SMART, COOK SMART TIPS:

* Any variety of kale can be used for this recipe. It is fun to experiment with green curly kale, lacinato or dinosaur kale and red/purple kale.
* Be sure to buy nut butters with only 1-2 ingredients: the nuts and maybe salt, that's it!
* Don't forget to zest the lime before cutting it up to squeeze for the juice.
* I finely chop the kale stems and add them to our weekly salad mix, add them to my mirepoix (carrot, celery and onion) when making soup or throw them into stir-fries.

Thai Inspired Kale Chips

Kale is EVERYWHERE these days! That is fantastic news, since it is one of the most nutrient-dense foods on the planet! This recipe is a great way to enjoy kale as a flavorful snack. Kale chips are starting to show up in little packages in the grocery store, but can be pricey. You can make you own in minutes and the flavor combination will having you grabbing one crispy bite after another. You won't believe that you are eating a green leafy veggie!

INGREDIENTS

1 large bunch of raw kale (any variety)*

1 Tablespoon almond butter or peanut butter*

1 ½ teaspoon Date Syrup pg296 or maple syrup

1 lime (zest and juice)*

¼ teaspoon soy sauce or gluten-free tamari (if avoiding gluten)

dash of cayenne pepper, chili garlic sauce or Sriracha (optional)

PROCEDURE

1. Rinse the kale under cool running water, rip bite sized pieces of the leaves off of the stems and let them soak in a large bowl of ice water for 5-10 minutes (or up to several hours if you are busy with other tasks). Reserve the stems for later use.*

2. Dry the kale with a salad spinner or by wrapping in paper towel. Preheat oven to 280°F.

3. In a small bowl, whisk the nut butter, syrup, lime zest, lime juice, and soy sauce/tamari until well combined. If you like your kale chips spicy, be sure to add your favorite "heat" – cayenne pepper, chili garlic sauce or Sriracha.

4. In a large bowl, combine the kale and sauce, using your hands to "massage" the kale, which will help breakdown the kale a bit while also making sure the each piece is well coated.

5. Spread the kale on parchment lined baking sheets, in a single layer, being careful not to crowd the pieces and bake for ~10-15 minutes at 280°F. The chips are ready when they are very dry and crispy, but can burn and then taste bitter, so begin checking them after 8-10 minutes, depending on your oven.

Popsicle Bar

THIS IS A TWO-PART BAR, SINCE IT TAKES SEVERAL HOURS TO OVERNIGHT FOR THE POPSICLES TO FREEZE. IT IS A FANTASTIC WAY TO GET THE KIDS INVOLVED PREPARING TASTY COOL TREATS THAT CAN HELP KEEP THEM HYDRATED, REFRESHED AND FUELED WITH WHOLE FRUIT.

Basic Bar

Use little paper cups, fill ¾ full, cover with foil and pierce the foil with wooden popsicle stick so that it stays in place while freezing.

LIQUID OPTIONS:

Your favorite smoothie

Fresh squeezed juice

Raising the Bar

Purchase a few different plastic reusable popsicle molds

"Instant Popsicle Machine" – special fluid filled metal mold that you freeze the night before and then it produces a few popsicles "on the spot" (~5 minutes)

LIQUID OPTIONS:

Herbal tea (chilled or cold brewed)

Sweet Lemon Base:
Puree zest of 1 lemon and flesh of 2 lemons + 5-6 pitted Medjool dates soaking in 8-12 oz of water + all soaking water

Orange You-Lee-Us Base:
Puree 1 teaspoon of zest and all of the flesh of 1 large orange + 2 pitted Medjool dates soaking in 8-12 oz of water + soaking water + ½-1 teaspoon vanilla extract

Refreshing Fruit Soup Foodie Bar pg208

Triple Power Smoothie pg186

FRUIT OPTIONS:

(cut into small pieces to fit easily into popsicle molds)

Strawberries, Raspberries, Blackberries, Blueberries

Pomegranate arils

Banana, cut each slice into quarters

Kiwi

Mango

Papaya

Pineapple

Peach/Nectarine

Mandarin/tangerine sections, cut into 3-4 pieces

Cherries, chopped small

Grapes, chopped into quarters

Fresh mint, finely chopped

Hummus Bar

LINE UP YOUR FOOD PROCESSORS, MINI CHOPPERS AND HAVE A HUMMUS SHOWDOWN!

Basic Bar

INGREDIENTS:

Garbanzo beans

Sesame seeds

Lemons

Fresh garlic (or granulated garlic powder)

Cumin, ground

Parsley, fresh or dried

DIPPERS:

Whole grain crackers

Carrots, celery and cucumber

Raising the Bar

INGREDIENTS:

Sun-dried tomatoes

Roasted red peppers

Olives, green and Kalamata are most flavorful

Roasted Garlic pg228

Capers, with brine (liquid from jar)

Cilantro, fresh (instead of parsley)

Italian Seasoning pg278

Lime juice and zest (instead of lemon)

Green and Black Olive Tapenade pg262

DIPPERS:

Raw red, orange and yellow sweet bell peppers

Jicama Chips pg242

Fennel (cut into sticks like celery)

Zucchini rounds or sticks

Broccoli or Cauliflower florets (raw or lightly steamed and chilled)

Radish rounds

Seasoned Pita Chips pg156

Mia's 1-2-3 Easy Tortilla Chips pg154

MAJOR BONUSES – YOU SCORED!

* Make your own hummus salad dressing!!! Simply thin out your favorite hummus recipe with equal parts of water and vinegar (apple cider vinegar, red wine vinegar or balsamic vinegar) and add some spicy brown or Dijon mustard (start with a few teaspoons and add more based on flavor preference) and ground black pepper.
* Hummus freezes like a champ! Just keep the amount that you'll use over the next few days in the fridge and freeze the rest in small containers.

MY OWN ADDITIONS OR IDEAS/RECIPES TO TRY:

_____

_____

_____

FAVORITE INGREDIENTS/COMBINATIONS:

_____

_____

WHO LOVED THIS FOODIE BAR?

_____

SET UP THIS FOODIE BAR AT WHICH SPECIAL EVENTS/PARTIES/POTLUCKS?

_____

NEXT TIME I MAKE THIS FOODIE BAR, I WILL:

_____

_____

RECIPE USED IN THESE BARS:

**Mediterranean Fajita
Foodie Bar**

Dilla Foodie Bar

*SHOP SMART, PREP SMART, COOK SMART TIPS:

* Traditional hummus recipes use tahini, a sesame seed butter/paste that can be quite expensive to purchase at the store. I like making it easy and going right to the source – sesame seeds! I always keep some sesame seeds in my freezer to use in a variety of recipes.
* Using fresh garlic in this recipe is wonderful, but if you are not a garlic-lover yet, start out with a small clove of garlic in this recipe, as the flavor will get stronger by the next day and you can always add more!
* To maximize the amazing power of garlic's phytonutrients, be sure to press it (through a garlic press) or chop it well and let it sit for at least 10 minutes before adding heat or acid (e.g. salsa, sauce, marinade, soup or dressing with citrus, tomato, vinegar).
* Be sure to zest citrus fruits BEFORE cutting them into pieces to squeeze the juice. A microplane is my favorite zesting tool, and we want the zest, as it may prevent skin cancer!

Go-To Hummus

When I met my husband, I quickly came to understand that there were certain textures that he had decided not to eat, one being custard (pudding, flan, custard are all out) and the other being what he would call "mushy" – in this group he includes oatmeal, tapioca, lentils and hummus. He has always enjoyed guacamole and black bean dips, go figure?! I am not exactly sure what possessed him to try my homemade hummus, but when he did, he was pleasantly surprised and now enjoys it whenever we happen to have some in the fridge. I love to eat it with a variety of veggie dippers slathered in our wraps (kale or collard leaves, or whole grain tortillas), on sandwiches made with whole grain bread or whole wheat pitas, and it does amazing work in my famous Humm-adillas. AND – BIG BONUS: it freezes perfectly, so double the recipe and stash a container or two in the freezer!

INGREDIENTS

1 ½ cups of cooked garbanzo beans, reserve ~⅓ cup liquid from cooking or can (1 can -14.5 oz)

Juice from 1 lemon (use some or all of the zest* if you like a pronounced lemon "bite")

¾-1 teaspoon cumin, ground

1 Tablespoon sesame seeds*

1-2 cloves* garlic, pressed or minced*

2 Tablespoons fresh parsley (or 1 teaspoon dried parsley)

~2 Tablespoons water (or reserved liquid from garbanzo beans)

Our favorite extras:

1-2 teaspoons capers, with brine (liquid in jar)

1-2 Tablespoons sun-dried tomatoes, chopped small

2-3 olives, if needed for saltiness

PROCEDURE

1. Press the garlic and let it sit for 10 minutes while you gather the rest of the ingredients.

2. Combine all ingredients in food processor and start out pulsing to get everything moving.

3. Continue to process until desired texture is achieved, adding more water/liquid if it is too thick.

*SHOP SMART, PREP SMART, COOK SMART TIPS:

*   Toast walnuts in a dry pan over medium heat, just until they begin to smell great, don't burn them!
*   I use the food processor to make cracker crumbs out of 100% whole grain crackers without any partially hydrogenated fats (or any type of added oil).

Muhammara-mus

Muhammara is a delicious spread or dip made from roasted red peppers and walnuts that I added garbanzo beans to in order to make my hummus-like "Muhammara-mus"! While the name is quite silly, the flavors are fantastic! It is a satisfying snack, with crunchy veggies, a spread for a roll/wrap, and can even be turned into a salad dressing by thinning it with your favorite vinegar and a bit of water… Yum!!! Adjust the seasonings to your liking, as there is a lot of room to "turn up the heat" if you like it hot!

INGREDIENTS

12 oz. jar of roasted bell peppers, drained

½ cup walnuts, lightly toasted

½ cup hemp seeds or sunflower seeds (or a combination)

⅔ cup crushed whole grain cracker crumbs* or Homemade Croutons pg254

Juice and zest from a fresh lemon

1-2 garlic cloves (pressed, crushed or minced)

½ teaspoon cumin (add more to taste)

½ teaspoon coriander (add more to taste)

¾ cup garbanzo beans (½ of a 14 oz. can)

1 Tablespoon hot sauce of your choice (add more to taste)

2 teaspoons Date Syrup pg295, or maple syrup

Salt/pepper to taste (add after you have tasted it)

PROCEDURE

1. In a food processor using an "s" blade, pulse a few handfuls of crackers/croutons at a time until you have a total of ⅔ cup of fine crumbs.

2. Then, add the drained roasted peppers and the remainder of the ingredients to the cracker crumbs in the food processor. Process until desired texture is achieved.

3. Add a dash of black pepper and more hot sauce (or a sprinkle of salt), based on taste preferences.

4. Will keep in the refrigerator for a week and freezes very well, so you might want to put a small container of it in the freezer to enjoy in a few weeks!

Recipe adapted by The Nutrition Professor from www.onegreenplanet.org

Baked Chip Bar

Basic Bar

INGREDIENTS:

Corn Tortillas (store-bought) – organic if available

Whole Wheat Pitas

Whole Wheat Lavash

Lime

Lemon

[Clean spray bottle with water if you don't have any limes or lemons]

Taco seasoning

Garlic powder (granulated garlic)

Chili powder

Cayenne pepper, ground

Cumin, ground

Coriander, ground

Raising the Bar

INGREDIENTS:

Austin's Smoky Spicy Blend pg276

Savory Spice Blend pg280

Italian Seasoning pg278

Fresh parsley, finely chopped

Fresh cilantro, finely chopped

Scallions, finely chopped

Minced onion, dried

Coconut sugar

Smoked paprika

Curry powder

Hot sauce

Nutritional yeast (for a slightly cheesy flavor)

Almond or soy milk

WACKY COMBINATIONS TO TRY

Lime juice + Sriracha + granulated garlic/powder + dusting of coconut sugar + cilantro

BBQ sauce thinned with water and brushed on tortillas + garlic powder + dried minced onion + smoked paprika + dried parsley

Italian Seasoning (use lemon juice)

Curry Powder (use lemon/lime or try almond or soy milk)

MY OWN ADDITIONS OR IDEAS/RECIPES TO TRY:

_____

_____

_____

_____

FAVORITE INGREDIENTS/COMBINATIONS:

_____

_____

_____

WHO LOVED THIS FOODIE BAR?

_____

SET UP THIS FOODIE BAR AT WHICH SPECIAL EVENTS/PARTIES/POTLUCKS?

_____

NEXT TIME I MAKE THIS FOODIE BAR, I WILL:

_____

_____

RECIPE USED IN THESE BARS:

Nacho Foodie Bar
Zuna Foodie Bar
Hummus Foodie Bar
Cowboy Salad Foodie Bar
Guacamole Foodie Bar
Salsa Foodie Bar

154

Mia's 1-2-3 Easy Tortilla Chips

My kids are bona fide chip-lovers! I, on the other hand, do not want them to consume all of that oil, so I decided to make my own super crunchy chips! These are so easy that you may wonder why you didn't start making them sooner. They also stay good for several days to a week in an air-tight container at room temperature. This version is my daughter's favorite.

INGREDIENTS

4 corn tortillas, organic (if available)

1 lime

Taco seasoning (store-bought) or Austin's Smoky Spicy Blend pg276

PROCEDURE

1. Cut the lime in half and rub around the entire top surface of 2 corn tortillas and sprinkle evenly with seasoning.

2. Cut the tortillas into quarters and then each quarter in half to make eight triangles.

3. Bake at 350-375° F for 5-10 minutes* until crispy all of the way through, but not dark.

175°C

*SHOP SMART, PREP SMART, COOK SMART TIPS:

* Depending on your oven, it might be best to go with a lower temperature and a longer cooking time to avoid burned chips! You may also need to move pans around while they bake if you have hot spots in your oven.

* We have a convection oven which blows hot air around, so the chips tend to cook pretty quickly. I also like to bake our chips on pizza screens (available very inexpensively at any local restaurant supply) which are super light and allow air to travel well.

RECIPE USED IN THESE BARS:

Zuna Foodie Bar
Hummus Foodie Bar
Guacamole Foodie Bar
Salsa Foodie Bar

156

Seasoned Pita Chips

It is nearly impossible to find baked pita chips in the supermarket that do not have oil as a major ingredient, so I just make my own. They would stay well for a few weeks in an airtight container, that is, if they weren't eaten up so quickly with hummus and guacamole!

INGREDIENTS

Whole wheat pita bread

Fresh lemon

Taco seasoning (store-bought) or Savory Spice Blend pg280

PROCEDURE

1. Preheat oven to 350°F and line a baking sheet with parchment paper or use a pizza screen.

2. Cut the pita bread in half across the middle and then separate each top from the bottom.

3. Cut the lemon in half and rub around the entire surface of one side of each of the 4 pieces of pita and sprinkle evenly with seasoning.

4. Cut each of the pita halves into four triangle shaped chips.

5. Bake at 350-375°F for 5-10 minutes* until crispy all of the way through, but not dark.

*SHOP SMART, PREP SMART, COOK SMART TIPS:

* Since you don't want to burn these chips, and all ovens heat a little bit differently, it might be best to go with a lower temperature and a longer cooking time. You may also need to flip pans around, or move them between racks, while they bake if you have hot spots in your oven.

* I like to bake our pita chips on pizza screens (available very inexpensively at any local restaurant supply) which are super light and allow air to travel well, which works especially well, since we have a convection oven which blows hot air around. If I don't watch these carefully, they'll get too dark before I know it!

Sweet Cinnamon Chips

These remind me of the little pieces of leftover pie crust that my mom used to dust with cinnamon and sugar and bake for my sister and me, except that these are ready in just minutes and a much kinder recipe to your body, inside and out! We love to pile them with fruit and my chocolate sauce pg286 to make AMAZING dessert nachos pg200!

INGREDIENTS

Whole grain Lavash Bread

Almond milk or soy milk

Coconut sugar or date sugar mixed with cinnamon

PROCEDURE

1. Preheat oven to ~350-375°F (convection is super). Brush each large lavash bread with a little almond milk or soy milk, making sure to get the full area, so that the cinnamon/sugar mixture will stick.
2. Sprinkle with cinnamon sugar mixture on lavash and THEN cut each large lavash into chip-size pieces.
3. Transfer to a parchment lined baking sheet or pizza screen and bake ~5-10 mins, or just until crispy, being careful not to let them burn.
4. Let cool completely on a wire rack. These light and crispy chips store well in a an airtight container for at least a week.

*SHOP SMART, PREP SMART, COOK SMART TIPS:

* I always buy a few extra packages of the lavash bread and freeze it. I cut the lavash in half and then make 3 packs with 4 lavash pieces wrapped in plastic wrap and put back into the original zip-top bag. The smaller size is easier to store without getting damaged – e.g. corners broken off, and when the plastic wrap covers well, it will help to prevent freezer burn.
* Be sure to brush on the soy or almond milk and sprinkle the cinnamon-sugar mixture before cutting the lavash into chip-size pieces.

Cowboy Salad Bar

I HAVE BEEN MAKING COWBOY SALAD FOR YEARS, AND WHEN I CHANGE UP THE INGREDIENTS, IT RESULTS IN VERY DIFFERENT FLAVORS, SO IT WORKS WELL FOR A BAR. GET SOME FRIENDS TOGETHER AND TASTE TEST EACH CREATION.

Basic Bar

INGREDIENTS:

Tomato-based salsa, any flavor* (store bought) OR tomatillo-based salsa, any flavor* (store bought)

Lemon (zest* and juice) or lime (zest* and juice)

Corn, frozen

Beans, canned, rinsed and drained

Avocado

DIPPERS:

Bell pepper strips

Zucchini rounds

Cucumber round

Carrot rounds

Celery boats

Whole grain crackers/chips

Raising the Bar

INGREDIENTS:

Homemade Salsa (see Salsa Foodie Bar pg174) or Makayla's Fire Roasted Salsa pg178

Beans, cooked from dry

Red onion, diced small

Corn, fresh from cob

Fresh cilantro, chopped small

DIPPERS:

Jicama Chips pg242

Mia's 1-2-3 Easy Tortilla Chips pg154

MAJOR BONUSES – YOU SCORED!

* Use your Cowboy Salad as a filling for delicious wraps made from lettuce, cabbage, steamed collard greens, or whole grain tortillas, just top with the addition of chopped fresh greens, sweet bell pepper and shredded carrot.
* Turn your Cowboy Salad into a dressing – either use it "as is" (this is one of my husband's favorite dressings for our Crazy Salad pg72), or add mustard and some apple cider vinegar (that is how I prefer to enjoy it on my salad).

MY OWN ADDITIONS OR IDEAS/RECIPES TO TRY:

_____

_____

_____

FAVORITE INGREDIENTS/COMBINATIONS:

_____

_____

WHO LOVED THIS FOODIE BAR?

_____

SET UP THIS FOODIE BAR AT WHICH SPECIAL EVENTS/PARTIES/POTLUCKS?

_____

NEXT TIME I MAKE THIS FOODIE BAR, I WILL:

_____

_____

RECIPE USED IN THESE BARS:

Crazy Salad Foodie Bar
Loaded Potato Foodie Bar

162

T's Cowboy Salad

While it is especially good with fresh corn in the summer, frozen organic corn is so easy to find that I love making it all year round! It is amazingly versatile and keeps well for at least a week in the refrigerator. Whether you serve it as a salad dressing*, as a dip with jicama chips pg242, mini sweet bell peppers, raw zucchini, cucumber cut into rounds, whole grain chips, or in a wrap with a whole grain tortilla, with chopped fresh spinach and shredded carrots, it might just become a family favorite at your house, too!

INGREDIENTS

1 avocado

24 fl oz jar of your favorite salsa

1 cup of corn (fresh from 2 ears or frozen)

3 cups of cooked beans (or 2 cans, rinsed and drained)*

1 lime – zest AND juice*

PROCEDURE

Combine all ingredients in a large bowl, making sure to zest the lime before squeezing it for it's juice.

*SHOP SMART, PREP SMART, COOK SMART TIPS:

* Choose 50% less sodium beans (or cook your own beans!)
* Always zest your citrus whole with a Microplane, before cutting into quarters to juice.

Fruit Skewers Bar

THIS IS A VERY FUN BAR TO SET UP FOR ENTERTAINING, AS EACH PERSON CAN BRING ONE TYPE OF FRUIT AND THE HOST CAN MAKE THE SAUCES. IT IS ALSO INTERACTIVE AND A CROWD PLEASER FOR ALL AGES!

Basic Bar

INGREDIENTS:

Apple chunks
Strawberries
Banana pieces
Blueberries
Grapes, seedless

DRIZZLE OPTIONS:

Squeeze juice from a fresh orange wedge over each skewer and dust with cinnamon

Raising the Bar

INGREDIENTS:

Kiwi
Mango
Papaya
Raspberries
Blackberries
Pears
Mandarin/tangerine sections
Starfruit
Peach/Nectarine chunks
Pineapple

DRIZZLE OPTIONS:

T's Dreamy Chocolate Sauce pg286
Date Night Caramel Sauce pg288
Dazzle-Berry Sauce pg290
Sweet Mango Lime Sauce pg292

MY OWN ADDITIONS OR IDEAS/RECIPES TO TRY:

_____

_____

_____

_____

FAVORITE INGREDIENTS/COMBINATIONS:

_____

_____

_____

WHO LOVED THIS FOODIE BAR?

_____

SET UP THIS FOODIE BAR AT WHICH SPECIAL EVENTS/PARTIES/POTLUCKS?

_____

NEXT TIME I MAKE THIS FOODIE BAR, I WILL:

_____

_____

Frozen Grape Kabobs

This simple preparation for grapes turns the already delicious fruit into an irresistible snack for kids and adults, alike. While we enjoy them any night of the week, to satisfy that evening "sweet tooth", the skewers make this recipe perfect for a party. The preparation will be done ahead of time, so they will be at your fingertips when guests want a sweet treat. Since it is difficult to rush through eating them frozen, everyone has fun savoring each grape!

INGREDIENTS

Ripe table grapes (your favorite variety or combination of varieties)

Bamboo skewers*

Gallon zip-top freezer bags

PROCEDURE

1. Rinse the grapes in a colander and remove from stems, transferring to a bed of paper towels to remove excess moisture.

2. Fill each skewer* with grapes, alternating colors, if using different varieties.

3. Place skewers in gallon zip-top bags and store in freezer until ready to eat – do not thaw before serving, as the grapes can "over" soften.

*SHOP SMART, PREP SMART, COOK SMART TIPS:

* Remove the sharp ends of the bamboo skewers, after loading them up with grapes, if they won't fit in the freezer bag without poking through. You can also skip the skewer altogether and simply freeze the rinsed (and dry de-stemmed) grapes in a freezer bag.

167

Guacamole Bar

Basic Bar

INGREDIENTS:

Avocado

Lime or Lemon (zest* and juice)

Salsa (store bought)

Granulated Garlic/Powder

Hot Sauce (if desired)

Salt/pepper (to taste)

Raising the Bar

INGREDIENTS:

Homemade salsa (see Salsa Foodie Bar pg174)

Jalapeño or serrano pepper, diced (seeds and ribs removed unless you like heat)

Chipotle in adobo*

Tomato, diced small

Garlic, fresh pressed or roasted

Fresh cilantro, finely chopped

Scallions, finely chopped

Red onion, diced

Pureed cooked beans and/or peas

Chili powder

Cayenne pepper, ground

Cumin, ground

Coriander, ground

Austin's Smoky Spicy Blend pg276

Savory Spice Blend pg280

Fiery Fruit Salsa pg176

Makayla's Fire Roasted Salsa pg178

Fruit: pomegranate arils, pineapple, watermelon, orange, mango, strawberries, kiwi

DIPPERS:

Jicama Chips pg242

Sweet Bell Pepper Strips (red, orange, yellow)

Baked Sweet Potato Fries pg222

Zucchini planks

Carrot sticks

Cucumber rounds

Mia's 1-2-3 Easy Tortilla Chips pg154

Seasoned Pita Chips pg156

*SHOP SMART, PREP SMART, COOK SMART TIPS:

* Be sure to zest citrus fruits BEFORE cutting them into pieces to squeeze the juice. A microplane is my favorite zesting tool, and we want the zest, as it may prevent skin cancer!
* To maximize the amazing power of garlic's phytonutrients, be sure to press it (through a garlic press) or chop it well and let it sit for at least 10 minutes before adding it to the guacamole, since it contains tomatoes and lemon juice (acids).
* Chipotle in adobo can be found canned or jarred in nearly every supermarket and adds a smoky flavor. The seeds in these roasted jalapeños are very spicy, so be sure to keep them out of your guacamole if you don't like a lot of heat!

MY OWN ADDITIONS OR IDEAS/RECIPES TO TRY:

_____

_____

FAVORITE INGREDIENTS/COMBINATIONS:

_____

WHO LOVED THIS FOODIE BAR?

_____

SET UP THIS FOODIE BAR AT WHICH SPECIAL EVENTS/PARTIES/POTLUCKS?

_____

NEXT TIME I MAKE THIS FOODIE BAR, I WILL:

_____

_____

RECIPE USED IN THESE BARS:

Burrito Bowl Foodie Bar
Loaded Potato Foodie Bar
Nacho Foodie Bar
Dilla Foodie Bar

Beany Guac

My daughter loves this version of guacamole because the beans mellow out the spicy flavors and cut the avocados' richness in your mouth, while also making this a substantial snack.

INGREDIENTS

1 avocado

1 cup beans, light colored* (cooked from dry or canned and rinsed)

½ cup tomato, diced

1 small garlic clove, pressed/minced*

2 Tablespoons fresh cilantro, chopped

2 Tablespoons fresh jalapeño, minced (use gloves and don't touch your eyes/face as it will burn!)

2 Tablespoons lemon juice (and ~¼-½ teaspoons zest*)

salt/pepper (to taste)

PROCEDURE

Combine all ingredients except for avocado in food processor and process until beans are as smooth as possible, add the avocado and pulse until well combined.

*SHOP SMART, PREP SMART, COOK SMART TIPS:

* To maximize the amazing power of garlic's phytonutrients, be sure to press it (through a garlic press) or chop it well and let it sit for at least 10 minutes before adding it to the guacamole, since it contains tomatoes and lemon juice (acids).
* Be sure to zest citrus fruits BEFORE cutting them into pieces to squeeze the juice. A microplane is my favorite zesting tool, and we want the zest, as it may prevent skin cancer!

Greeny Guac

My husband and son swear that they can't stand the texture or flavor of green peas, but when I made this recipe, they proceeded to eat nearly the entire batch for lunch! I don't think that we need to advertise that it contains peas, just make it and enjoy!

INGREDIENTS

2 avocados

1 cup green peas, thawed from frozen

1 medium tomato, diced

1 small garlic clove, pressed/minced*

1 large scallion, green and white parts, chopped

⅛ teaspoon cayenne pepper, ground (or more to taste)

¼ cup fresh cilantro, chopped

1 lime – all of the juice (and ~¼-½ teaspoons of zest*)

salt/pepper (to taste)

PROCEDURE

Combine all ingredients except for avocado in food processor and process until as smooth as possible, add the avocado and pulse until well combined.

*SHOP SMART, PREP SMART, COOK SMART TIPS:

* To maximize the amazing power of garlic's phytonutrients, be sure to press it (through a garlic press) or chop it well and let it sit for at least 10 minutes before adding it to the guacamole, since it contains tomatoes and lime juice (acids).
* Be sure to zest citrus fruits BEFORE cutting them into pieces to squeeze the juice. A microplane is my favorite zesting tool, and we want the zest, as it may prevent skin cancer!

Salsa Bar

HAVE A BLAST MAKING A WHOLE BUNCH OF DIFFERENT SALSAS. LET YOUR TASTE BUDS AND IMAGINATION LEAD THE WAY! THIS IS A FUN BAR TO DO ALONG WITH THE BAKED CHIP BAR (PG152) AND ANY LEFTOVER SALSA CAN EVEN BE INCORPORATED INTO A GUACAMOLE BAR (PG168) THE NEXT DAY!

Basic Bar

INGREDIENTS:

Tomatoes, diced small

Lime or lemon

Red onion and/or scallion, chopped small

Green chilis, fire roasted

Garlic, fresh or granulated garlic powder

Chili powder

Cumin, ground

salt/pepper (to taste)

Raising the Bar

INGREDIENTS:

Tomatillos, diced small

Jalapeño (fresh or pickled)*

Chipotle in adobo*

Fresh cilantro, finely chopped

Cayenne pepper, ground

Coriander, ground

Austin's Smoky Spicy Blend pg276

Savory Spice Blend pg280

Roasted Garlic pg228

Hot Sauce

Fruit: Pineapple, mango, strawberries, papaya, kiwi, peach/nectarine, plum, orange

DIPPERS:

Jicama Chips pg242

Sweet bell pepper strips (red, orange, yellow)

Zucchini planks

Carrot sticks

Cucumber rounds

Mia's 1-2-3 Easy Tortilla Chips pg154

Seasoned Pita Chips pg156

*SHOP SMART, PREP SMART, COOK SMART TIPS:

* Chipotle in adobo can be found canned and jarred in nearly every supermarket. The seeds in these roasted jalapeños are very spicy, so be sure to keep them out of your salsa if you don't like a lot of heat!
* Jalapeño seeds and white ribs are the hottest part, so don't put those in your salsa unless you like it hot!

MY OWN ADDITIONS OR IDEAS/RECIPES TO TRY:

_____

_____

_____

FAVORITE INGREDIENTS/COMBINATIONS:

_____

_____

WHO LOVED THIS FOODIE BAR?

_____

SET UP THIS FOODIE BAR AT WHICH SPECIAL EVENTS/PARTIES/POTLUCKS?

_____

NEXT TIME I MAKE THIS FOODIE BAR, I WILL:

_____

_____

Fiery Fruit Salsa

This is a fun salsa to make because it combines red tomatoes and green tomatillos with two summer fruits that we get to enjoy all year long, thanks to our freezers!

INGREDIENTS

¼ cup pineapple (fresh or thawed from frozen*), diced small

¼ cup mango (fresh or thawed from frozen*), diced small

¼ cup tomatillos, diced small

¼ cup tomato, diced small

¼ – ½ teaspoons lime zest* + 1 Tablespoon fresh lime juice

⅛ teaspoon chili powder (or more to taste)

PROCEDURE

Combine all ingredients a bowl, stir well and enjoy!

*SHOP SMART, PREP SMART, COOK SMART TIPS:

* While many people assume that fresh produce is always superior to frozen, when it comes to many fruits, this just isn't the case. Mangoes, for example, are often sold unripe and may take many days to ripen on the countertop. Frozen mangoes, on the other hand, are picked at the peak of their ripeness (and sweetness) and frozen within just a few hours.
* This is a great recipe to get some experience with tomatillos, since their tartness is well balanced by the sweet fruit.
* Be sure to zest citrus fruits BEFORE cutting them into pieces to squeeze the juice. A microplane is my favorite zesting tool, and we want the zest, as it may prevent skin cancer!

© Makayla Hopkins

RECIPE USED IN THESE BARS:

Burrito Bowl Foodie Bar
Nacho Foodie Bar
Cowboy Salad Foodie Bar
Guacamole Foodie Bar

*SHOP SMART, PREP SMART, COOK SMART TIPS:

* While the thought of roasting all of the vegetables together may be appealing, the liquid from the tomatoes can cause the onions, peppers and garlic to "steam or boil" rather than roast and ultimately develop the caramelized flavor.
* Zest the lime before squeezing for an extra punch of lime flavor!
* Whether you experiment with growing your own tomatoes for the first time, have earned a reputation for growing amazing tomatoes, or simply buy tomatoes at the farmers' market, this is a great recipe to double, triple or quadruple!
* Play around with including different peppers, based on heat preference from mild to smokin' hot: bell peppers, Anaheim, Poblano, Jalepeño, Serrano, Cayenne, Aji, Pequin, Thai Chili, Jamaican Hot pepper, Habanero, Scotch Bonnet.

Makayla's Fire Roasted Salsa

I had the honor of having Makayla Hopkins, the Founder/Farmer of Scarlet's Farm and blog fitfarmer14.wordpress.com in one of my NUTRI 300 classes at Cosumnes River College. She is currently a nutrition and dietetics student at Chico State and not only is she an amazing farmer, she is a great cook and quite the photographer! This is what she wrote about her delicious salsa recipe...

"Being able to experience the taste of each ingredient in its entirety is what separates a good salsa from a GREAT salsa. This recipe packs a punch and calls you back for more! Have fun growing the peppers, tomatoes, and cilantro in a small-scale garden and explore the simplicity and beauty of truly fresh salsa." ~Makayla

INGREDIENTS

3 tomatoes, chopped

¼ red onion, chopped

3 garlic cloves, sliced in half

1 small jalapeño pepper, seeded and sliced

1-2 serrano* peppers, seeded and sliced

¼ cup chopped cilantro

Juice* of 1 lime

Dash of Himalayan sea salt

PROCEDURE

1. Preheat oven to 425-450°F and place chopped tomatoes in a baking dish and the garlic, jalapeño and onion in a separate* baking dish.

2. Put both baking dishes in the oven for 10-15 minutes or until slightly roasted, stirring to ensure that the garlic doesn't burn.

3. Let cool for at least 3-5 minutes, then transfer ingredients (except cilantro and salt) to the food processor and pulse 4-6 times.

4. Add fresh lime juice and cilantro, and pulse an additional 2-3 times, or until the texture is just the way you like it! Add salt to taste, if desired.

BEVERAGE BARS

Smoothie Bar

SMOOTHIES ARE A CONVENIENT WAY TO ENJOY A VARIETY OF FRUITS & VEGETABLES. MAKING THEM AT HOME SAVES MONEY AND GIVES YOU THE CHANCE TO GET A LITTLE CREATIVE!

Basic Bar

(Aim for at least ½ cup of veggies for every cup of fruit)

FRUIT OPTIONS:

Berries – blackberries, blueberries, raspberries, strawberries (fresh or frozen*)

Kiwi (with or without skin)

Pineapple

Apple and pears (leave skin on – but discard seeds)

Banana, fresh or frozen

Citrus fruit (can include zest or entire peel – white pith and seeds can be bitter) – oranges, Mandarins, tangerines

Stone fruit (with skin but pit removed) – peaches, nectarine, cherries, dates

Grapes – red, black, green

Melon – watermelon, cantaloupe, honeydew

VEGETABLE OPTIONS:

Leafy greens: kale, spinach

Carrot, cucumber, celery

Herbs: parsley, mint

NUT/SEED/LEGUME OPTIONS:

Walnuts, peanut butter (~ 1 Tablespoon)

Chia seeds, flax seeds (2-3 teaspoons)

Silken tofu (~3 oz)

LIQUID OPTIONS:

Water (and ice)

Plant milk – almond milk, soy milk

Coconut water

Raising the Bar

Experiment a little! Try adding a few of the options below, putting in 1 cup of veggies for every ½ cup of fruit and finding the combinations that taste the best!

FRUIT OPTIONS:

Berries – cranberries, boysenberries (fresh or frozen*)

Pomegranate arils (fresh or frozen*)

Persimmons

Citrus fruit (can include zest or entire peel – white pith and seeds can be bitter)- lemons, limes, grapefruit, kumquats*

Stone fruit (with skin but pit removed)- apricots, plums, mango, jujube

Melon – casaba, canary, Crenshaw, Galia

VEGETABLE OPTIONS:

Leafy greens – mixed greens, romaine lettuce, red or green leaf lettuce, chard, collard greens, turnip greens, mustard greens, dandelion greens

Broccoli, Fennel, ginger, beets, turmeric root

Herbs- cilantro, basil

NUT/SEED/LEGUME OPTIONS:

Beans (any kind), cooked from dry or canned and rinsed – start with 2 Tablespoons

Almond butter (1 Tablespoon)

GRAIN OPTIONS:

Start with a Tablespoon and add more if desired

Cooked brown rice, oatmeal (cooked or raw), bulgur (cooked/rehydrated)

*SHOP SMART, PREP SMART, COOK SMART TIPS:

* Fresh blackberries, blueberries and raspberries go bad (mold) so ridiculously fast that I nearly always buy them frozen. If I go to a berry farm and come home with a large amount, I will freeze them on baking sheets and then move them to freezer zip-top bags until I want to use them for a smoothie, fruit crisp or other recipe.
* Kumquats- Roll each kumquat between your palms for 10 seconds or so to enhance their sweetness. The skin is sweet and inside is sour, so you don't want to peel them before adding them to your smoothie, may be just cut them in half and pop out any large seeds.
* To "cook" bulgur, add enough boiling water to reach ~1 inch above the bulgur, cover with a plate or plastic wrap and a dish towel and let stand 30 minutes.

* Lemon zest contains phytonutrients with anti-cancer potential, so you might want to experiment with leaving the peel on 1 or both lemons (may change the flavor a bit).
* No need to peel the ginger, just clean it well, as precious nutrients lie just beneath the very thin, papery skin.
* If possible, purchase organic varieties of fruits and veggies, but especially greens, celery and cucumber for this recipe, as when conventionally grown, these can have detectable pesticide residue.

Jenni's "Migraines Are No Fun" Smoothie

One of my closest friends, Jenni Frisk, has suffered from way too many migraines. One morning at the gym, we were talking about what she could do to help and I suggested including more greens, as those phytonutrients are so important for optimizing the health of our blood vessels and circulation. She thought that adding a daily green smoothie would be very doable and started a blog to document her efforts to reduce the frequency of her migraines https://youcantarguewithcrazy.wordpress.com She went from having several each week to 204 days without a migraine!

INGREDIENTS

3 cups leafy greens (Jenni's favorites: spinach and baby kale)

¾ cup coconut water

2 stalks celery

~½ cucumber (or more)

1-2" piece of fresh ginger root

2 lemons, peeled*

1 cup frozen pineapple

PROCEDURE

Combine all ingredients in a blender (a high-powered one works best), in the order listed. Blend until very smooth.

Jenni's advice: "Separate into two portions, one for today and one for tomorrow, unless you are battling a migraine, then I drink ½ in the morning and ½ in the afternoon."

Triple Power Smoothie

This delicious smoothie unites three of the most beneficial foods on the planet – berries, green and beans. You won't even realize that you are celebrating the power of GREENS and BEANS as you enjoy sip after sip! This quick recipe can be ready in a few minutes as you fly out the door in the morning, as an after work (or after workout) snack or split it with someone you love, as a sweet treat at the end of the evening!

Makes 1 smoothie (~2 cups) – be sure to double the recipe if you are making it for more than 1 person.

INGREDIENTS

½ banana, fresh or frozen*

1 mandarin orange (or ½ of a "regular" sized orange)

½ cup frozen berries*

½ cup frozen pineapple or 1 kiwi

2 Tablespoons white beans, cooked (from dry or canned and rinsed)*

1 cup raw kale*

1 cup water

2-3 ice cubes (optional – if you like it slushy)

PROCEDURE

Combine all ingredients in a blender and blend until smooth.

*SHOP SMART, PREP SMART, COOK SMART TIPS:

* While bananas ripen well at room temperature, if a banana is perfectly ripe before you are ready to eat it, put in into the fridge. The outer skin will darken, but the banana itself will not get soft for several days. When bananas get too ripe, just peel them and slice them in half or into small chunks and freeze them (I keep a gallon-size zip-top freezer bag stocked with bananas).
* Frozen berries should be a staple in your house, they are ready on the fly and don't mold, like fresh berries can!
* Cooked beans freeze extremely well, so I freeze them in ¼-½ cup quantities in zip-top bags or small plastic storage containers.
* Experiment with all different types of greens in your smoothies!

*SHOP SMART, PREP SMART, COOK SMART TIPS:

* Ceylon is the healthiest variety of cinnamon (available online)
* Organic silken tofu can be purchased in convenient, shelf-stable, aseptic boxes and kept in the pantry until opened.

Wildly Delicious Strawberry Smoothie

This refreshing drink is a great way to start the morning if you are short on time or to refuel after a workout! Smoothie recipes are very flexible, so feel free to substitute your favorite seasonal fruits. Don't be "afraid" of using tofu in this smoothie. The important phytonutrients will go right to work in your cells and all that you will taste is creamy deliciousness! I always add a handful or more of greens to my smoothies for an extra boost of nutrients, just be aware that the color will change.

INGREDIENTS

½ cup strawberries, fresh or frozen

1 orange

1 ripe banana, fresh or frozen

½ apple (unpeeled, core removed)

6 oz of silken tofu* – ½ box

1 teaspoon cinnamon*

1-2 teaspoons flax seed

4 fluid oz water

Add ice based on texture/temperature preference

Leafy greens, a handful or more – just start with a few leaves!

PROCEDURE

1. Add all ingredients to your blender, soft fruits and liquid at bottom and blend until very smooth.
2. Add ice through lid, while blending, if desired. Enjoy each and every sip!

Watermelon Refresher

Picking the fantastic watermelon is quite an art... heavy for it's size, dull skin, nice big yellowed "field spot" where the melon has been resting in the sun ripening on the vine, but it still seems like a gamble! When you crack into one and the flesh is not quite as firm as you had hoped, it may be just perfect for this drink! Mint, cucumber, lime and watermelon complement each other nicely, for a very clean taste and fun way to help stay hydrated. The highest levels of available antioxidants, especially lycopene, in watermelon are found right after it has been cut from whole, before being refrigerated. Be sure to use the white part of the rind, too! It is packed with phytonutrient goodness!

INGREDIENTS

1 ½ cups watermelon (with white rind*)

¾ cup cucumber

2-4 Tablespoons fresh mint

1 lime, zest* and juice

Ice cubes, based on taste preference

2 teaspoons chia seeds (optional)

PROCEDURE

Combine all ingredients in blender and enjoy, adding as little or as much ice as desired.

*SHOP SMART, PREP SMART, COOK SMART TIPS:

*   Enjoy as much of the white rind as possible, as it contains many helpful phytonutrients, including an amino acid that has been shown to improve blood circulation, just discard the very green outer layer of skin.
*   Be sure to zest citrus fruits BEFORE cutting them into pieces to squeeze the juice. A microplane is my favorite zesting tool, and we want the zest, as it may prevent skin cancer!

Flavored Water Bar

I DRINK WATER ALL DAY LONG, AND SOMETIMES I FORGET HOW THE SIMPLE ADDITION OF FRUIT AND HERBS CAN MAKE ME FEEL LIKE I AM AT A SPA!

Basic Bar

INGREDIENTS:

Filtered water

Cucumber rounds

Fresh mint

Lemon slices

Lime slices

Orange slices

Pineapple, small pieces (fresh or frozen)

Raising the Bar

INGREDIENTS:

Apple slices

Strawberries (fresh or frozen)

Blueberries (fresh or frozen)

Raspberries (fresh or frozen)

Blackberries (fresh or frozen)

Kiwi slices

Mango chunks (fresh or frozen)

Papaya chunks

Pomegranate arils (fresh or frozen)

Starfruit slices

Peach/nectarine chunks (fresh or frozen)

Melon, any variety (fresh or frozen)

Fresh basil

Fresh parsley

MAJOR BONUSES – YOU SCORED!

* Keep your flavored water in a large pitcher or 32 fluid ounce glass jar in the refrigerator, so that you will have it at your fingertips.
* Make ice cubes from fresh or frozen fruit and herbs, in standard ice cube trays or the specialty silicone shapes. These are a great option for party, since they are easy, but pretty fancy!

MY OWN ADDITIONS OR IDEAS/RECIPES TO TRY:

_____

_____

_____

*SHOP SMART, PREP SMART, COOK SMART TIPS:

* When you want some warmth in your cup, drink your hot tea with lemon or plain, since cow's milk and soy milk have been shown, at least in test tubes, to block some of the tea's beneficial impact on blood vessel cells.

* Although tea has been shown to reduce iron absorption by as much as 50% when consumed with a meal, Vitamin C can triple iron absorption. So, drink your tea with lemon or enjoy Vitamin C rich foods at mealtime (red bell peppers, broccoli, citrus fruits, kiwis, strawberries). If you have anemia, you might want to curtail tea and coffee drinking for an hour before and during meals, and stick with sipping tea in between meals.

Timaree's Tropical Splash

When it comes to maximizing the antioxidant power of tea, longer brewing time is better than shorter, and cold beats out hot, by a long shot, since hot water can destroy some of the beneficial compounds. So, the very best, and easiest, way to prepare tea with the highest level of antioxidant potential is cold steeping in the fridge. Before you go to bed, take a few minutes to prepare this delicious drink that you can sip all day long (up to 32 fluid oz), as it provides a very unique opportunity to stay hydrated while also getting a boost of flavor and powerful antioxidant nutrients without any calories! If you are sipping plain water, you just might be missing out!

INGREDIENTS

7 ½ to 8 cups of water (depending on size of pitcher/container)

Juice of 1 lemon

½ cup fresh or frozen pineapple chunks (or pineapple canned in it's own juice – not syrup)

4 tea bags (look for hibiscus as the first ingredient on the label – Lemon Zinger is a favorite!)

PROCEDURE

1. Combine all of the ingredients in a large pitcher with lid or 64 fl oz mason jar.

2. Refrigerate overnight, remove tea bags in the morning and enjoy!

3. This will keep for several days in the refrigerator, with the fruit flavor intensifying each day.

DESSERT BARS

Dessert Nacho Bar

DON'T WAIT UNTIL YOUR NEXT PARTY TO CELEBRATE WITH THIS DESSERT NACHO BAR, SET ONE UP SOON!

Basic Bar

CHIPS:

Apples, sliced into thin wedges (use as "chips")

Banana, cut in rounds then in quarters

Strawberries, small dice

TOPPINGS:

T's Dreamy Chocolate Sauce pg286

Chopped Pecans

Toasted Coconut (unsweetened)

Raising the Bar

CHIPS:

Sweet Cinnamon Chips pg158

Pineapple cut into semi-thin pieces to resemble chips

Crisp pear, sliced into thin wedges for chips

TOPPINGS:

Blueberries, Raspberries, Blackberries (fresh or frozen)

Kiwi, small dice

Pomegranate arils (fresh or frozen)

Peaches or nectarines, small dice

Mango or papaya, small dice

Cherries, pitted, small dice (fresh or frozen)

Pineapple, diced small

Pear, diced small

Mandarin orange sections, cut into small pieces

Chopped almonds, walnuts, pistachios, hazelnuts or macadamia nuts

Dusting of cinnamon and cayenne (if you like a little heat)

SAUCES:

Date Night Caramel Sauce pg288

Dazzle-Berry Sauce pg290

Sweet Mango Lime Dessert Sauce pg292

MY OWN ADDITIONS OR IDEAS/RECIPES TO TRY:

_____

_____

_____

_____

FAVORITE INGREDIENTS/COMBINATIONS:

_____

_____

_____

WHO LOVED THIS FOODIE BAR?

_____

SET UP THIS FOODIE BAR AT WHICH SPECIAL EVENTS/PARTIES/POTLUCKS?

_____

NEXT TIME I MAKE THIS FOODIE BAR, I WILL:

_____

_____

✴ SHOP SMART, PREP SMART, COOK SMART TIPS:

* Since the Sweet Cinnamon Chips pg158 stay crisp in an air-tight storage container, I end up making them once a week or so, and try to keep extra whole wheat lavash bread in the freezer since they are ready in just minutes.

* Toast a small amount of nuts in a dry saucepan (or use a baking sheet in the oven for larger batches), just until they begin to smell delicious, as you do not want them to burn. Keep the pecans whole, if possible, so that they will roast evenly. Once cooled, they can easily be chopped up and sprinkled on your favorite foods or stored in a small container in the freezer.

Sweet Nachos for Breakfast

My kids' response to this recipe…"Dessert Nachos for breakfast?! Seriously? This is awesome!" they exclaimed, as I prepared a gorgeous plate that not only tastes great, but will also fuel them all morning. Bring some fun into your morning routine with this easy recipe that everyone can help assemble.

INGREDIENTS

Sweet Cinnamon Chips pg158 (6-10 per person)

Banana, sliced and quartered

Strawberries, diced small

Blueberries

T's Dreamy Chocolate Sauce pg286

Date Night Caramel Sauce pg288

Toasted* pecans, chopped*

Toasted coconut, unsweetened

PROCEDURE

1. Start with a layer of chips on each plate, add a generous amount of banana, strawberries and blueberries.

2. Then, don't be shy about drizzling T's Dreamy Chocolate Sauce and/or Date Night Caramel Sauce all over the chips and fruit.

3. Top with pecans and coconut and enjoy right away!

Mom's Apple Berry Nachos

I love apples and berries and this recipe is just downright fun! I also like to add in kiwi and banana when I have them on hand.

INGREDIENTS

Apple, cut into very thin slices (only thick enough to be used as chips)

Blueberries (frozen)

Strawberries, diced small

Dazzle-Berry Sauce pg290

Toasted* pecans, chopped*

PROCEDURE

1. Layer the apples slices on a plate and top with strawberries and blueberries.
2. Then, drizzle on a generous amount of Dazzle-Berry Sauce pg290 and top with lightly toasted pecans and enjoy every bite!

*SHOP SMART, PREP SMART, COOK SMART TIPS:

* If you start cutting the apple, get pulled away to another task, and when you return the pieces have browned, don't worry! Between the fruit toppings, sauces and nuts, you'll have a gorgeous and delicious finished product.
* Toast a small amount of nuts in a dry saucepan (or use a baking sheet in the oven for larger batches), just until they begin to smell delicious, as you do not want them to burn. Keep the pecans whole, if possible, so that they will roast evenly. Once cooled, they can easily be chopped up and sprinkled on your favorite foods or stored in a small container in the freezer.

Oatmeal Cookie Bar

OATMEAL COOKIES ARE MY FAVORITE AND I LOVE PLAYING AROUND WITH DIFFERENT INGREDIENTS TO CHANGE UP THE FLAVORS.

Basic Bar

INGREDIENTS:

¼ cup old fashioned oats

1 ¾ cup old fashioned oats, ground into flour

1 teaspoon aluminum-free baking powder

½ teaspoon baking soda

½ cup beans (cooked from dry or canned and drained, liquid reserved)

½ cup coconut sugar (or other unrefined dry sweetener)

¼ cup unsweetened applesauce

¼ teaspoon cinnamon (see other spice options below)

½ teaspoon vanilla extract (see other extract options below)

STIR-IN OPTIONS:

⅓ cup semi-sweet chocolate chips (dairy-free)

½ cup raisins

Raising the Bar

SWEETENER OPTIONS:

In place of coconut sugar – use ⅔ cup date sugar and add a few Tablespoons of additional liquid – water or almond milk

STIR-IN OPTIONS:

Grated carrot

Grated apple

Dried pineapple, diced small

Dried peaches, diced small

Dried apricots, diced small

Dried blueberries

Walnuts, chopped

Almonds, chopped

Pistachios, chopped

MAJOR BONUSES – YOU SCORED!

* These cookies freeze fabulously – in fact, if I don't keep them in the freezer (out of sight, out of mind), I might eat them, ALL! My husband warms them in the oven for a few minutes, while I like to eat them right out of the freezer.

* This cookie dough can also be frozen before it is cooked. Simply scoop out the dough onto a parchment lined baking dish/pan/screen that will fit into the freezer. Press to flatten each cookie, as if you were going to bake them, but then cover lightly with plastic wrap and freeze until solid (for a few hours to overnight). Transfer that frozen cookie dough into a gallon zip-top freezer bag. Whenever you are ready, bake a handful of them directly from the freezer. (You may need to add an extra minute or two to the baking time.)

SPICE/EXTRACT OPTIONS:

Chai Spice Blend pg282

Pumpkin Pie Spice pg284 (store bought or see recipe)

Lemon extract (stronger flavor than vanilla, so start with ¼-½ teaspoon)

Almond extract (stronger flavor than vanilla, so start with ¼-½ teaspoon)

GENERAL PROCEDURE FOR OATMEAL COOKIES:

1. Preheat oven to 350°F. Line baking sheet with parchment paper and set aside.

2. Put 1 ¾ cup of the oats in a high-powered blender or food processor and pulse, about 15x, until crumbly but not fine powder. Transfer to a mixing bowl and combine with baking powder, baking soda, salt, and spice(s). Whisk to incorporate and set aside.

3. Drain beans, reserving liquid. Put beans in blender or food processor with applesauce, coconut sugar (or date sugar), vanilla extract (or other extract) and 1 Tablespoon of the bean liquid. Whiz until smooth.

4. Pour wet mixture into dry mixture and stir about 10 times. Add mix-ins, remaining ¼ cup oats and more of the bean liquid, as needed, stirring until combined. If the mixture is too wet, add more oats. If it's too dry, add a few teaspoons of bean liquid, water or almond milk/soy milk.

5. Drop Tablespoons of batter onto the parchment lined cookie sheet, leaving an inch of room between each cookie. Bake 15 minutes, until edges are just turning light brown and middles are set. They will firm a bit more as they cool. Check the bottoms to make sure they are golden brown.

*SHOP SMART, PREP SMART, COOK SMART TIPS:

*   They freeze amazingly well, as does the scooped and ready to bake dough. Just freeze it on parchment paper and then transfer to a zip-top freezer bag or place in plastic food storage container with plastic wrap in between layers to keep dough scoops from freezing together.
*   I always make a triple batch which uses an entire can of white beans, 2 little plastic tubs of applesauce and made 52 good sized cookies (#40 scoop).
*   Make these cookies gluten-free by using certified gluten-free oats.

Oatmeal Chocolate Chip Cookies

Oatmeal chocolate chip cookies are easily my FAVORITE cookie! They are so tempting, that I need to keep the cookies (or the unbaked cookie dough) in the freezer, or I will eat one every time I walk into the kitchen! These cookies have one of my most cherished "secret" ingredients of all times, beans… Don't tell anyone, just let them enjoy the wonderful treats!

INGREDIENTS

¼ cup old fashioned oats*

1 ¾ cup oat fashioned oats* ground into flour (use high-powered blender or food processor)

1 teaspoon aluminum-free baking powder

½ teaspoon baking soda

¼ teaspoon cinnamon

dash of ground cardamon (optional)

dash of salt

½ cup canned white beans, liquids reserved

½ cup coconut sugar (can also substitute ⅔ cup date sugar, may need extra moisture – water or juice)

¼ cup unsweetened applesauce

½-1 teaspoon vanilla extract

⅓ cup chocolate chips (dairy-free)

PROCEDURE

1. Preheat oven to 350°F. Line baking sheet with parchment paper and set aside.

2. Put 1 ¾ cup of the oats in a high-powered blender or food processor and pulse, about 15x, until crumbly but not fine powder. Transfer to a mixing bowl and combine with baking powder, baking soda, salt, cinnamon and cardamon. Whisk to incorporate and set aside.

3. Drain beans, reserving liquid. Put ½ cup of beans in blender or food processor with applesauce, coconut sugar, vanilla extract and 1 Tablespoon of the bean liquid. Whiz until smooth.

4. Pour wet mixture into dry mixture and stir about 10 times. Add chips, remaining ¼ cup oats and more of the bean liquid, as needed, stirring until combined. If the mixture is too wet, add more oats. If it's too dry, add a few teaspoons of bean liquid, water or apple juice.

5. Drop Tablespoons of batter onto the parchment lined cookie sheet, leaving an inch of room between each cookie. Bake 15 minutes, until edges are just turning light brown and middles are set. They will firm a bit more as they cool. Check the bottoms to make sure they are golden brown.

Recipe adapted by The Nutrition Professor from www.drmcdougall.com by Mary McDougall.

Refreshing Fruit Soup Bar

THE POSSIBILITIES FOR DELICIOUS COMBINATIONS ARE VIRTUALLY ENDLESS! IT IS PERFECT FOR MAKING WITH KIDS, SINCE TASTING IS KEY, INGREDIENTS ARE FEW, IT CAN BE PLATED WITH PIZAZZ AND IS READY TO BE ENJOYED RIGHT AWAY OR CHILLED FOR LATER. MY KIDS LIKE TO FREEZE PART OF THE BATCH IN POPSICLE MOLDS. COMBINE THE FOLLOWING INGREDIENTS IN A FOOD PROCESSOR OR POWERFUL BLENDER, AND BLEND UNTIL SILKY SMOOTH! BE SURE TO TASTE AS YOU GO!

Basic Bar

INGREDIENTS:

Melon: Any variety will do! Cantaloupe, Honeydew, Watermelon

Citrus: Lime, lemon, orange – use some (or all) of the fruits' zest, and juice.

Extra sweetness (if needed): Tasting is critical. Some melons are so sweet that you'll skip this step, however, if you want to add a little boost of sweetness, go for a whole food source:

1-2 soft, pitted Medjool dates blend perfectly and add extra fiber and health-promoting phytonutrients.

Raising the Bar

INGREDIENTS:

Melon: Try different varieties or combinations – Crenshaw, Ambrosia, Galia, Cantadew…

Citrus: Experiment with grapefruit, blood oranges or tangerines – use some zest and juice.

Flavor bursts: Fresh mint or even basil? Some fresh jalapeño (avoid seeds) or a pinch of cayenne will create a sweet-spicy flavor profile!

Creamy touch: A splash of soy milk or almond milk can bring a hint of creamy richness to the soup.

GARNISH TO YOUR HEARTS CONTENT!

Mint sprigs

fresh or frozen berries

a dash of cayenne or cinnamon

thin slices of citrus

MAJOR BONUSES - YOU SCORED!

* Enjoy some of the best popsicles ever by freezing these soups in plastic popsicle molds or small paper cups.
* Make a slushy dessert by freezing in ice cube trays and then using a food processor to puree or pour into a frozen dessert machine!
* Have fun with 2 different melon soups served in the same bowl or cup!

MY OWN ADDITIONS OR IDEAS/RECIPES TO TRY:

_____

_____

_____

FAVORITE INGREDIENTS/COMBINATIONS:

_____

_____

WHO LOVED THIS FOODIE BAR?

_____

SET UP THIS FOODIE BAR AT WHICH SPECIAL EVENTS/PARTIES/POTLUCKS?

_____

NEXT TIME I MAKE THIS FOODIE BAR, I WILL:

_____

_____

Sweet Galia Soup with a Hint of Heat

Here is an example of how I used my Refreshing Fruit Soup Bar to make a delicious soup with a Galia melon. It would be wonderful with any other green fleshed melon, so have fun experimenting! It can be enjoyed for breakfast, a snack or even dessert!

INGREDIENTS

A large honeydew (or other green fleshed melon) peeled and chopped into large chunks

1-2 dates (if needed for extra sweetness)

1 lime – use zest and juice

1 small handful of mint (amount based on taste preference)

¼ small jalapeño (seeds removed) or dash of cayenne

Splash of almond milk (amount to vary based on desired thickness of the soup)

Garnish: fresh or frozen blackberries and mint

PROCEDURE

Combine all of the ingredients (except for the garnish) in a food processor or very powerful blender. If you use a traditional blender, you may need to add more liquid, so the soup may have a thinner consistency.

Cantadew Soup with Orange and Mint

Here is another product of our Refreshing Fruit Soup Bar with a Cantadew melon. Any other orange fleshed melon would also be excellent, so enjoy experimenting!

INGREDIENTS

A large cantaloupe (other orange fleshed melon) peeled and chopped into large chunks

1-2 dates (based on the natural sweetness of the melon)

1 Mandarin orange or ½ "regular" size orange – use zest and orange flesh with juice

1 small handful of mint (amount based on taste preference)

dash of cayenne

Splash of soy milk (amount to vary based on desired thickness of the soup) – almond milk works great, too!

Garnish: fresh or frozen raspberries and mint

PROCEDURE

1. Combine all of the ingredients (except for the garnish) in a food processor or very powerful blender.
2. After I zested the orange, I peeled it and then instead of squeezing it for juice, I just added the whole fruit right to the food processor.
3. If you use a traditional blender, you may need to add more liquid, so the soup may have a thinner consistency.

MORE RECIPES

RECIPE USED IN THESE BARS:

Scramble Foodie Bar

Mediterranean Fajita Foodie Bar

Crazy Salad Foodie Bar

Pizza Foodie Bar

Loaded Potato Foodie Bar

Pasta Foodie Bar

Dilla Foodie Bar

*SHOP SMART, PREP SMART, COOK SMART TIPS:

* While roasted or grilled bell peppers taste amazing, be sure to eat some of your sweet peppers raw, as quite a few of their nutrients are destroyed by heat (though other nutrients are more available to your body once the peppers have been cooked).
* Parchment Paper is WONDERFUL – since nothing sticks and it won't leave any chemicals in your food (just say "NO" to non-stick spray)!
* Be sure to zest citrus fruits BEFORE cutting them into pieces to squeeze the juice. A microplane is my favorite zesting tool, and we want the zest, as it may help prevent skin cancer!

Mediterranean Grilled Veggies

I love the flavor of roasted or grilled veggies, and how I cook them depends on how much I am making and the weather (too hot to cook in the kitchen or too cold/rainy to use the backyard BBQ). More often than not, I use my oven (roasting several baking pans full of vegetables at once) or, for a smaller amount ready in a flash, I use a countertop grill (George Foreman-type) or panini maker.

INGREDIENTS

Veggie Options:

Zucchini

Carrots

Potatoes

Sweet potatoes

Mushrooms

Red, yellow and orange bell peppers*

Red onions

Scallions

Eggplant

Turnips

Asparagus

Beets

Broccoli and Cauliflower

Fennel

Winter Squash (butternut, acorn, pumpkin...)

Brussels Sprouts

Green beans

Seasoning:

Italian Seasoning pg278

Splash of water or vegetable broth

Black pepper, ground

Optional Toppings:

Lemon zest* and little squeeze of juice

Parsley, fresh – chopped

Lightly roasted and crushed walnuts or pine nuts, – sprinkle on just before serving

PROCEDURE

1. Cut each type of vegetable into similarly-sized pieces, so that they will cook evenly (a big piece of carrot can take 2-3 times longer to cook than a smaller piece).

2. If the vegetables are dry, toss with just enough water or broth so that the seasonings will stick (Italian Seasoning and black pepper).

3. Pre-heat oven to 375°F and roast on baking pans lined with parchment paper* until tender-crisp.
   Alternatively, heat an indoor grill on med-high to high and cook until just tender and grill marks form. The vegetable pieces that are cut with similar shape (thickness) are especially important for even cooking when using an indoor grill.

RECIPE USED IN THESE BARS:

Burrito Bowl Foodie Bar
Nacho Foodie Bar
Crazy Salad Foodie Bar
Dilla Foodie Bar

*SHOP SMART, PREP SMART, COOK SMART TIPS:

* While roasted or grilled bell peppers taste amazing, be sure to eat some of your sweet peppers raw, as quite a few of their nutrients are destroyed by heat (though other nutrients are more available to your body once the peppers have been cooked).
* Parchment Paper is WONDERFUL – since nothing sticks and it won't leave any chemicals in your food (just say "NO" to non-stick spray)!
* Be sure to zest citrus fruits BEFORE cutting them into pieces to squeeze the juice. A microplane is my favorite zesting tool, and we want the zest, as it may prevent skin cancer!

Grilled / Roasted Fajita Vegetables

It seems that we can never have enough grilled/roasted vegetables in the fridge, as they get gobbled up in fajitas, tacos, burritos, wraps, grain dishes, sandwiches and more! This recipe is very similar to Mediterranean Roasted Veggies, as it only differs in the seasonings. My kids love Chipotle's fajita veggies (onion and green bell pepper), yet are often surprised by how easy my recipe is and how good they taste! Just like with my Mediterranean Roasted or Grilled Veggies, use your oven, backyard BBQ or countertop electric grill/panini maker.

INGREDIENTS

Veggie Options:

Zucchini

Carrots

Potatoes

Sweet potatoes

Mushrooms

Red, yellow and orange bell peppers*

Red onions

Scallions

Eggplant

Turnips

Asparagus

Beets

Broccoli and Cauliflower

Fennel

Winter Squash (butternut, acorn, pumpkin…)

Brussels Sprouts

Green beans

Seasoning:

Austin's Smoky Spicy Blend pg276 or taco seasoning (store-bought)

Splash of lime juice, water or vegetable broth

Optional Toppings:

Lime zest* and little squeeze of juice

Cilantro, fresh – chopped

Lightly roasted and crushed pumpkin seeds (pepitas) – sprinkle on just before serving

PROCEDURE

1. Cut each type of vegetable into similarly-sized pieces, so that they will cook evenly (a big piece of carrot can take 2-3 times longer to cook than a smaller piece).

2. If the vegetables are dry, toss with just enough water or broth so that the seasonings will stick.

3. Pre-heat oven to ~375°F and roast on baking pans lined with parchment paper* until tender-crisp.
   Alternatively, heat an indoor grill on med-high to high and cook until just tender and grill marks form. The vegetable pieces that are cut with similar shape (thickness) are especially important for even cooking when using an indoor grill.

* Steam frying is a wonderful technique to maximize flavor without using oil!
* Press or mince the garlic at least 10 minutes before using to maximize nutrient content of the finished dish.
* Chipotle peppers in adobo sauce can be purchased in a can or jar at the supermarket. They are hot, so be sure to remove the seeds if you like mild flavors, or use the peppers whole and remove before serving. Freeze individual peppers with a teaspoon of sauce in zip-top bags, as I have never found a recipe that uses an entire can!

RECIPE USED IN THESE BARS:

Burrito Bowl Foodie Bar
Loaded Potato Foodie Bar
Nacho Foodie Bar
Dilla Foodie Bar

Timaree's Seasoned Black Beans

These black beans come together in a hot minute, are a great "go-to" food to have in your fridge all week long (and even freeze well!)

INGREDIENTS

3 cups black beans (cooked from dry or canned, rinsed & drained)

1 small red onion, diced very small

2-3 cloves garlic, pressed/minced*

1 chipotle in adobo*, seeds removed and finely chopped (or left whole for less spicy beans)

1-2 teaspoons ground cumin

1-2 teaspoons ground coriander

½ teaspoons smoked paprika

1 ½ cup ripe tomatoes, chopped or 1 can fire roasted tomatoes with garlic

PROCEDURE

1. Steam "fry"* the onion in a saucepan on medium high heat, adding a few Tablespoons of water or broth when they begin to stick and brown.

2. When onion has softened and started to caramelize, adding garlic and cook for 30 seconds more.

3. Add chipotle pepper (if using chopped up), cumin, coriander, and smoked paprika and cook for 30 seconds while stirring.

4. If using chipotle whole (will be taken out at the end and result in a more mild dish), add chipotle, cooked black beans, and tomatoes.

5. Simmer for 5-20 minutes.

RECIPE USED IN THESE BARS:

Burrito Bowl Foodie Bar
Crazy Salad Bar
Nacho Foodie Bar
Dilla Foodie Bar

*SHOP SMART, PREP SMART, COOK SMART TIP:

* To maximize the health benefits of garlic, chop/press it and let it rest for 5-10 minutes before putting it in contact with acidic foods/liquids or heat.

Cauliflower Lentil Filling

The original recipe was recommended to me by a former student, who proceeded to tell me that she had made it five times over the past month or so, as her boyfriend loved it and would ask her to make it as soon as they finished off a batch. My family had the same reaction! I adjusted the seasoning to our liking and have been making it every other week for quite a while… no complaints! We use it in tacos, enchiladas, on nachos, in salad, wraps and more!

INGREDIENTS

3 cup water

1 cup dry lentils, sorted and rinsed (green lentils hold their shape well)

6 cloves garlic, minced* (divided – 2 cloves for the lentils, 4 cloves for the cauliflower)

1 large head cauliflower, cut into evenly sized flowerets, stem cut into similarly sized pieces

1 red onion, diced

Spice mix:

2-3 Tablespoons chili powder

¼-½ teaspoon chipotle chili powder (adobo)

1 teaspoon cumin

1 teaspoon smoked paprika

1 teaspoon salt-free mesquite seasoning, if available

1 teaspoon dried oregano

1 teaspoon salt, or to taste

Black pepper to taste

PROCEDURE

1. Combine the water, lentils and 2 cloves of garlic in saucepan, bring to a boil and then simmer for ~20 minutes, until lentils are tender.

2. While lentils are cooking, use a food processor (or box grater) to cut the cauliflower into very small pieces (size of rice), being careful not to puree it.

3. In a pre-heated dry pan, cook onions until golden and translucent, using a bit of water or vegetable broth if they stick, though browning is important.

4. Add the spices and 4 cloves of minced garlic, and cook for ~30 seconds - 1 minute, stirring constantly before adding the cauliflower in batches, to facilitate adequate mixing (cauliflower should be well coated with spices).

5. Cook until just tender and then add cooked lentils.

Recipe adapted by The Nutrition Professor from www.http://blog.fatrfree.vegan.com

RECIPE USED IN THESE BARS:

Mediterranean Fajita Foodie Bar

Burrito Bowl Foodie Bar

Oven-Roasted Sweet Potato Fries

Within the first few days of purchasing sweet potatoes, I will scrub several, and then, leaving the skins on, cut them into wedges or "fries" and transfer them to a gallon zip-top bag and add seasoning. If I don't cook them right away, I put the bag in the bottom drawer of the fridge.

INGREDIENTS

Sweet potatoes (a variety of sweet potatoes, with both light and dark colored-flesh), cut into wedges/planks

Your favorite seasoning

Austin's Smoky Spice Blend pg276 or Savory Spice Blend pg280

Splash of water, aquafaba or veggie broth

PROCEDURE

1. Cut the sweet potatoes into wedges or "fries" (do NOT peel them) and transfer them to a gallon zip-top bag.

2. Add a splash of water, aquafaba, or veggie broth and a favorite bold seasoning.

3. Preheat oven to 400-425°F and line a baking sheet or two with parchment paper, give a bag a few good shakes to be sure the seasoning has been well distributed and spread them out into an uncrowded single layer, roast (turning once, halfway through, after about 12 minutes) until brown on both sides!

RECIPE USED IN THESE BARS:

**Mediterranean Fajita
Foodie Bar**

Burrito Bowl Foodie Bar

Pizza Foodie Bar

Loaded Potato Foodie Bar

Dilla Foodie Bar

*SHOP SMART, PREP SMART, COOK SMART TIPS:

* To quickly prepare the collards for cooking, rinse them, remove each stem and then roll the leaves up together and cut across the roll into thin ribbons. Chefs refer to this type of cut as "chiffonade".
* Do not overcook the collards, as the greens can toughen.

Really Quick Sautéed Collard Ribbons

If you would like start your collard adventure with a very mellow flavored, REALLY quick cooking recipe (cooking time: 1 minute) – try this! I made a few adjustments to a recipe that was originally published by Fine Cooking, that I found on a GREAT website: www. thebittenword.com The combination of malt vinegar and maple syrup might sound a bit odd, but it tastes wonderful!!!

INGREDIENTS

¼ orange or lemon (fresh)

½ Tablespoon malt vinegar

1 teaspoon maple syrup (or date syrup pg295)

1 bunch collard greens, cut into ribbons*

1-2 Tablespoons vegetable broth (in place of olive oil)

1-2 small cloves garlic, lightly smashed and peeled (use more garlic if you are a fan!)

Pinch crushed red pepper flakes

Kosher salt

PROCEDURE

1. Toss the collard ribbons with a generous squeeze of fresh lemon or orange juice and set aside.

2. In a small bowl, whisk the malt vinegar and maple syrup.

3. Heat the broth in a skillet over medium-high heat, add the garlic and cook until just lightly browned.

4. Remove the garlic with a slotted spoon/fork and set aside.

5. Add the pepper flakes to the hot pan, and immediately add the collards and ¼-½ teaspoon salt (optional).

6. Stir/toss the collards for about 1 minute* (greens will be bright to dark green and slightly wilted).

7. Add the garlic back into the pan with the greens, drizzle on the maple-vinegar mixture, stir well, and enjoy right away!

RECIPE USED IN THE BAR:

Crazy Salad Foodie Bar

*SHOP SMART, PREP SMART, COOK SMART TIPS:

* As soon as you get fresh beets home, be sure to cut the greens off, right at the top of the beet root, and store them in a separate bag. That way, the greens will not pull moisture away from the beets while they are waiting for you in the refrigerator!

* Thoroughly rinse any sand or debris from beet greens, dry in salad spinner or on paper towel. Chop the most tender leaves into shreds to add to salad greens, and/or chop any of the larger leaves to sauté with garlic and onion, for a separate dish.

* An easy way to have juice at your fingertips for any recipe, is to keep a container of juice concentrate (no added sugar), in your freezer. Apply the 3 parts water 1 part concentrate principle. For this recipe, since you needed ¼ cup of juice – use 1 Tablespoon orange juice concentrate mixed with 3 Tablespoons water.

Roasted Beets with Citrus

When you enjoy a big scoop of this delicious combination of citrus and beets on top of your favorite green salad, you won't need to use any other dressing!

INGREDIENTS

1 bunch of beets*

2 small oranges

Orange zest

1 garlic clove

½ teaspoons black pepper

¼ teaspoons salt

2 Tablespoons apple cider vinegar (can add more to taste)

¼ cup orange juice*

1 teaspoon maple syrup (or Date Syrup pg296)

1 teaspoon spicy brown mustard

PROCEDURE

1. Scrub beet roots well, wrap in parchment paper, then in foil, and roast on a foil lined baking sheet at 375°F for ~45-60 minutes or until tender (test by piercing with a knife).

2. While beets are roasting, zest the oranges and combine the zest with the reminder of ingredients: garlic, black pepper, salt, vinegar, orange juice, maple syrup and mustard.

3. Dice the oranges and stir them in.

4. Once beets are cool enough to handle, skin will easily rub off. Then, dice roasted beets into small pieces and add to orange/dressing mixture.

5. This will keep well in the refrigerator for a week.

RECIPE USED IN THESE BARS:

Pasta Foodie Bar

Zuna Foodie Bar

Salad Dressing (Shaken) Foodie Bar

Pesto Foodie Bar

Kale Chip Foodie Bar

Hummus Foodie Bar

Salsa Foodie Bar

Roasted Garlic

If you roast a whole bunch of garlic at one time, you can freeze the bounty and you will have roasted garlic at your fingertips... ready to make a salad dressing or Mia's Garlic Trees pg230 (or any other recipe that uses roasted garlic - see index), any night of the week!

INGREDIENTS

Several heads of garlic*

Parchment paper (cut into ~6″ squares)

Foil (cut into ~6″ squares)

PROCEDURE

1. Hold each head of garlic on it's side and carefully cut in half across the middle (widest point), being careful not to pull the top and bottom halves apart. Hold the head together, with the two halves still in place, and place in the middle of a square piece of parchment paper. Wrap the parchment paper up around the head of garlic and then surround with a piece of foil, to keep the parchment paper tightly wrapped around the garlic.

2. Roast at ~350°F until soft when gently squeezed (~30 minutes).

*SHOP SMART, PREP SMART, COOK SMART TIPS:

* When choosing garlic to purchase, pick firm heads, heavy for their size, without any signs of mold, sprouting or shriveling!
* I have been known to roast as many as 18 heads of garlic at one time! Once slightly cool, I squeeze out the delicious garlic into a bowl and then divide it into little bundles to freeze.

RECIPE USED IN THESE BARS:

Mediterranean Fajita
Foodie Bar

Burrito Bowl Foodie Bar

Pizza Foodie Bar

Crazy Salad Foodie Bar

Loaded Potato Foodie Bar

Mia's Garlic Trees

The hardest part of making this recipe for us seems to be getting the broccoli to the serving dish, as anyone who is in the kitchen with me can't stop eating it! I try to always have roasted garlic on hand, so that we can make Mia's Garlic Trees on a weeknight, when we are short on time.

INGREDIENTS

1 pound of raw broccoli, cut into bite-sized pieces

8-10 cloves of roasted garlic pg228

¼-⅓ cup veggie broth, warmed

1 Tablespoon nutritional yeast (optional)

Black pepper, to taste

PROCEDURE

1. Steam the broccoli until just barely tender, about 3-4 minutes.

2. Combine ¼ c of the broth* and roasted garlic cloves. Thoroughly smash garlic with a long-tined fork, to make a thick "sauce", adding a few more Tablespoons of the broth/water as needed, stir in nutritional yeast, if using.

3. Put the broccoli into the bowl with the roasted garlic sauce and gently mix to coat well. Season with black pepper to taste.

*SHOP SMART, PREP SMART, COOK SMART TIPS:

* You can roast garlic pg228 ahead of time, as it will last in the fridge for several days or tightly wrapped in the freezer for months. I often slip a packet or two of garlic cloves into the oven when I am cooking something else, so that I always have some in the freezer or fridge!
* In place of the broth, you can add 1-2 teaspoons of low sodium veggie broth base (paste) to ¼-⅓ cup of the water used to steam the broccoli.

RECIPE USED IN THESE BARS:

Mediterranean Fajita Foodie Bar

Burrito Bowl Foodie Bar

Pizza Foodie Bar

Crazy Salad Foodie Bar

Dilla Foodie Bar

*SHOP SMART, PREP SMART, COOK SMART TIPS:

* While asparagus is packed with vitamins, minerals and phytonutrients that keep our bodies healthy and strong, it only has 3 kcalories per spear... What a nutritional bargain!!!
* It is best to use asparagus within 1-2 days of purchasing it.
* To maximize freshness, store asparagus in the fridge, either in a vase with water, or with the ends wrapped in a damp paper towel.

2-min Broiled Asparagus

Not only is this recipe ridiculously easy and ready in a flash, but this fool-proof method for cooking asparagus will never let you down! Say goodbye to stringy or mushy asparagus spears, forever! Have the rest of your meal absolutely ready, before you put the asparagus in the oven, as it will only take a few minutes, especially if the spears are slender.

Mia's tip: My daughter loves to dip her asparagus in spicy brown or Dijon mustard!

INGREDIENTS

Fresh asparagus

Minced raw garlic or granulated garlic powder (not garlic salt)

Black pepper

PROCEDURE

1. Rinse the asparagus well, and remove the woody bottoms, (cut or broken off). Leave some water clinging to spears.

2. Arrange the asparagus on the baking sheet lined with parchment paper or foil, in a single layer so that spears do not overlap.

3. Sprinkle with black pepper and garlic powder. If using fresh, minced garlic, put the asparagus, garlic and pepper in a produce bag and gently shake/massage so that spears get coated with garlic, before transferring to the baking sheet.

4. Broil just until spears are tender to your liking... do NOT walk away from the oven, as your asparagus can over cook or the parchment paper even can catch on fire!

5. Serve immediately and enjoy every bite of asparagus goodness!

Timaree's Garlic Mushrooms

I make these mushrooms EVERY WEEK! We enjoy them in and on so many different dishes, including pizza, salads, wraps, pasta, grain dishes and more!

INGREDIENTS

24 oz of mushrooms, cleaned and sliced fairly thick

10+ cloves of garlic, crushed or minced

¼ cup – ½ cup vegetable broth

fresh parsley or Italian Seasoning pg278 (optional)

PROCEDURE

1. Brown mushrooms in a dry pan, in several batches, as it is very important not to crowd them. *(If the mushrooms overlap in the pan, they will end up steaming instead of browning. Another trick is not to disturb them until they have had a chance to brown, then flip them with a fork and brown on the other side.)*

2. Transfer browned mushrooms to a glass storage container and continue cooking the next batch.

3. Once all mushrooms have been browned, deglaze the pan with broth, add garlic and herbs/seasoning (if using).

4. Let the garlic cook for a few minutes, then add the mushrooms back into the pan, coat with garlic broth and cook for ~5 minutes on medium low.

5. Transfer back to the glass storage container and you will be able to enjoy grabbing these from the fridge throughout the week!

*SHOP SMART, PREP SMART, COOK SMART TIP:

* After crushing or pressing the garlic, let it sit for a 5-10 minutes before adding to the broth to maximize the cancer-fighting/preventing nutrients available to your body!

RECIPE USED IN THESE BARS:

**Mediterranean Fajita
Foodie Bar**

Pizza Foodie Bar

Dilla Foodie Bar

"Cook Smart" Caramelized Onions

Caramelizing onions in the oven is a cinch, so make a big batch (they can even be frozen)! Enjoy on sandwiches, salads, grain and bean dishes, pizza, wraps and more!

INGREDIENTS

4-5 red onions, slices of similar thickness*

1 Tablespoon balsamic vinegar

½ teaspoon salt (optional)

½ teaspoon pepper

PROCEDURE

1. Toss onions with vinegar, salt and pepper.
2. Arrange onions on 2 baking sheets lined with parchment paper.
3. Roast onions at 350°F until golden brown and sweet, about 30 minutes, stirring every 7-10 minutes to ensure even cooking.

*SHOP SMART, PREP SMART, COOK SMART TIPS:

* Red onions leave white and yellow onions in the dust when it comes to cancer fighting phytonutrients.
* To ensure even cooking, you will want to cut the onion into pieces that are about the same thickness. A very easy way to do this is to let the slicer blade of food processor do the work!

RECIPE USED IN THESE BARS:

**Mediterranean Fajita
Foodie Bar**

Pizza Foodie Bar

Crazy Salad Foodie Bar

Dilla Foodie Bar

Pickled Red Onions

Enjoy these delicious onions in any bean or green salad, in sandwiches, veggie burger and even on pizza! I keep a big jar in the back of my refrigerator.

INGREDIENTS

2 cup of cider vinegar

2 cup of water, room temperature or cold

3 Tablespoons coconut sugar or date sugar

1 teaspoon salt

1 teaspoon whole peppercorns

2 bay leaves

4 medium red* onions, thinly sliced

Fill a large pot with water, bring it to a boil

PROCEDURE

1. Combine the vinegar, 1 cup of water, coconut/date sugar, salt, and bay leaves in a medium sized bowl and stir until sugar dissolves.
2. Add the peppercorns in an empty "tea bag" or stainless steel tea infuser.
3. Place onion slices in colander in sink and pour all boiling water over onions (will wilt a bit).
4. Drain well and transfer onions to bowl with vinegar brine. Cover and allow to marinate at room temp for 1 hour and then refrigerate. I like to transfer the onions and marinade into glass canning jars.

Recipe adapted from Vegetable Dishes I Can't Live Without by Mollie Katzen.

*SHOP SMART, PREP SMART, COOK SMART TIPS:

* Red onions provide so many more amazing antioxidants than white or yellow onions, that I don't even bother buying any other type!
* Make a double batch, as they will keep in refrigerator for several weeks.

Smoky Spicy Corn

You may never think about corn the same again… This easy recipe quickly transforms mild corn into a taste sensation! My kids helped me adjust the seasonings, but play around with the amounts to suit your own preferences. You can make this corn as smoky or spicy as you'd like! It makes an incredible addition to so many recipes and as an item in a whole bunch of Foodie Bars!

INGREDIENTS

1 ½ cups corn (from 2 ear of fresh corn)*

½-1 teaspoon Austin's Smoky Spice Blend pg276

¼ teaspoon lime zest*

1 teaspoon lime juice (more based on taste preferences)

2-3 teaspoons fresh cilantro, chopped small

2-3 Tablespoons roasted sweet bell peppers (jarred or homemade) OR fresh, diced small (red, orange and yellow peppers work well)

Cayenne for sprinkling on top!

PROCEDURE

Combine all ingredients in a medium sized bowl and mix well.

*SHOP SMART, PREP SMART, COOK SMART TIPS:

* When purchasing fresh corn, it is important to find ears that are not dried/wilted/moldy. One tip is to pull down the husk and silk about 1-2 inches to expose the kernels. Each kernel should be plump with liquid. IF they are dry or moldy, find another ear to purchase.
* Buy organic corn whenever possible to reduce your exposure to GMO crops.
* Be sure to buy SMOKED paprika, not "regular" paprika, as they taste completely different!
* Be sure to zest citrus fruits BEFORE cutting them into pieces to squeeze the juice. A microplane is my favorite zesting tool, and we want the zest, as it may prevent skin cancer!

RECIPE USED IN THESE BARS:

Burrito Bowl Foodie Bar
Zuna Foodie Bar
Hummus Foodie Bar
Cowboy Salad Foodie Bar
Guacamole Foodie Bar
Salsa Foodie Bar

The Nutrition Professor's Jicama "Chips"

These jicama chips are one of my favorite snacks. They are crunchy and refreshing! We love to use them in place of tortilla chips at our house, so they get dipped into fresh guacamole, salsa and my husband and kids' all-time favorite – T's Cowboy Salad! pg162 They elevate jicama from "ok" to "I want more!"

INGREDIENTS

1 large jicama*

4-5 fresh lemons

Cayenne pepper, chili powder or your favorite hot sauce (optional)

PROCEDURE

1. Rinse the jicama and then peel it completely.
2. Slice into planks/chips into ¼" thick, and marinate in copious amounts of freshly squeezed lemon juice.
3. For a little kick, sprinkle citrus marinated jicama with your favorite chili powder or cayenne pepper.
4. Keep in the refrigerator in a gallon zip-top bag and enjoy it all week long! We pack it in our kids' lunches and I bring a baggie to work with my lunch.

*SHOP SMART, PREP SMART, COOK SMART TIPS:

* When purchasing jicama, look for those that are firm, heavy for their size and not coated in wax.
* This crunchy veggie blows chips away, as a cup offers nearly 4 times the fiber and a variety of vitamins and minerals all for only ⅓ of the kcals! The water and fiber in jicama will also go a long way towards helping you feel full and well hydrated!

The Quickest Apple Chips Ever

How many bites can you get out of one apple? Here is a creative way to mindfully enjoy every single bite of your next apple! Kids and adults alike will be amazed by how much "fun" eating an apple can be!

INGREDIENTS

1 apple, any size, any variety
Cinnamon*

PROCEDURE

Slice the apples as thin as possible, ideally using a mandolin/v-slicer, or with a very sharp knife and enjoy immediately!

*SHOP SMART, PREP SMART, COOK SMART TIPS:

* DON'T PEEL YOUR APPLES! Much of the amazing health-promoting, cancer-fighting nutrients are found in and just under the skin, so simply core the apples and you are ready to go!
* My favorite mandolin/v-slicer is made by Borner. I have had it for 20+ years and use it daily!
* Feel free to eat "naked" apple chips, or sprinkle with your favorite spice or spice blend – cinnamon, Pumpkin Pie Spice pg284 or Chai Spice Blend pg282.

RECIPE USED IN THESE BARS:

Mediterranean Fajita Foodie Bar

Crazy Salad Foodie Bar

*SHOP SMART, PREP SMART, COOK SMART TIPS:

* Whole lentils (green, brown, red or black) will take a bit longer to cook- ~30-45 minutes, though some will hold their shape, as these split-red lentils are very soft when cooked.
* My quick method for sorting all dried beans, peas and lentils is to spread the amount I am planning to cook on a clean baking sheet with sides (also known as a ½ sheet pan). This makes it easy to spot any little stones or twigs that would have tried to sneak into the pot!
* To maximize the amazing power of garlic's phytonutrients, be sure to press it (through a garlic press) or chop it well and let it sit for at least 10 minutes before adding heat or acid (e.g. salsa, sauce, marinade, soup or dressing with citrus, tomato, vinegar).
* Dial the heat up or down by the amount of crushed red pepper flakes to add.

Seasoned Lentils

Lentils are tiny but mighty! They are a member of the beloved legume family, but don't need to be soaked ahead of time and, depending on the variety, can cook up in under 15 minutes! These little gems look like tiny flying saucers or a lens and while most people think of them in soup (crockpot lentil soup is amazing), I enjoy lentils almost every day at lunch on my Crazy Salad pg72, pg70! I cook them up on Sunday so that they are at my fingertips all week long. Since I always have a delicious and very flavorful dressing on my salad, I typically do not add any of the seasoning options below when I make my lentils.

INGREDIENTS

1 cup split red lentils, sorted* and rinsed

2 ¼ cup water

¼ cup sherry (or your favorite cooking wine)

1 Tablespoon salt-free seasoning*

1 teaspoon black pepper, ground

1-2 cloves fresh garlic, pressed/crushed* or ½ teaspoon granulated garlic

⅛-¼ teaspoons crushed red pepper flakes*

Optional seasonings: Splash of reduced sodium soy sauce, gluten-free tamari or ~4 large green or Kalamata olives, finely chopped

PROCEDURE

1. Press the garlic and let it sit for 10 minutes while you sort* the lentils (see tip) and gather the rest of the ingredients.

2. Combine all ingredients, except for the lentils, in a 2-3 quart saucepan and bring to a boil.

3. Rinse the sorted lentils, stir into saucepan, cover with lid, reduce heat to simmer and cook, without lifting the lid) for ~12 minutes* or until tender.

4. Taste and then season, if desired, with reduced sodium soy sauce, gluten-free tamari or finely chopped olives.

RECIPE USED IN THESE BARS:

Burrito Bowl Foodie Bar
Crazy Salad Foodie Bar
Nacho Foodie Bar
Dilla Foodie Bar

*SHOP SMART, PREP SMART, COOK SMART TIPS:

* Some quinoa is pre-rinsed, package should indicate this.
* Toasting the quinoa is not necessary, but does tend to add a "nuttier" flavor to the dish.
* If not using V-8, increase water to 2 ¾ cups.
* For something extra special, pan sauté corn with onion, garlic, jalapeño and lime juice & zest.
* When I put the chopped greens (raw or frozen) at the bottom of a large stainless steel or glass bowl, then add the hot quinoa to the top, they cook/wilt just perfectly!

The Nutrition Professor's Mexican Quinoa

This tasty quinoa is fantastic as a taco/burrito filling, a topping for nachos when a cup of black beans are stirred in, will stay good in your fridge for a few days and can be frozen for use later!

INGREDIENTS

1 ½ cups uncooked quinoa, rinsed*

1 can low-sodium picante V-8*

1 ½ cups water

1-2 Tablespoons taco seasoning or Austin's Smoky Spice Blend pg276

2-3 cloves garlic, pressed or chopped very small

Mix-ins: scallions, corn*, black olives, cooked black beans, chopped leafy green (kale, chard, spinach) – either raw or frozen

PROCEDURE

1. Toast rinsed quinoa in dry saucepan*.
2. Add pressed/chopped garlic and taco seasoning and stir for 30 seconds. Do not let the garlic burn!
3. Then add V-8 and water, bring to a boil and reduce to simmer for 20-25 minutes.
4. Let rest for a few minutes, fluff with a fork and then carefully taste (temperature will be very hot).
5. Add extra seasoning if needed. Stir in any (or all) of the mix-ins that you desire.

Excellent Brown Rice Every Time

If you don't have a rice cooker, and tend to burn rice on the stove, this easy technique will produce excellent rice every time.

INGREDIENTS

1 ½ cups brown rice, uncooked (any variety)

Water

PROCEDURE

1. Add rinsed brown rice to a large pot of boiling water, stir it once, and cook uncovered for 30 minutes or until tender.

2. Drain rice for 15 seconds in a colander or sieve, then add it back to the pot, off the heat and put the lid on to allow it to steam for a few minutes.

*SHOP SMART, PREP SMART, COOK SMART TIP:

* If you like sticky white rice and have been disappointed with long grain brown rice in the past, give medium or short grain brown rice a try, as the texture is similar.
* Experiment with different types of brown rice, including Jasmine and Basmati, as well as other varieties of whole grain rice: wild, purple, black and red!
* Amazingly enough, compared to white rice, brown rice can have: 93% more Vit B-6, 280% more potassium, 450% more magnesium, 550% more fiber and 800% more Vit E!

RECIPE USED IN THE BAR:

Burrito Bowl Foodie Bar

Lime Cilantro Brown Rice

This recipe comes together in minutes and is fantastic next to my Seasoned Black Beans pg218 or in a burrito! Use your favorite chili pepper in place of the jalapeño. Try a Habanero if you like it really hot, a Serrano if you like it just a bit spicier, or a half of a Poblano or Pasilla, depending on the size, if you like it mild.

INGREDIENTS

⅓ cup scallions (green onions), finely chopped

1 jalapeño pepper, finely diced (~2 Tablespoons)

1-2 cloves fresh garlic, minced or pressed

a few Tablespoons of vegetable broth or tomato juice

2 Tablespoons lime juice, use 1 teaspoon of lime zest

3 Tablespoons fresh cilantro, finely chopped

½ teaspoon salt (optional)

3 cups cooked* brown rice (from 1 cup uncooked brown rice pg250)

PROCEDURE

1. Sauté scallions, jalapeño and garlic in broth or tomato juice for 2-3 minutes.
2. Stir in remaining ingredients, being sure to zest the lime before squeezing and warm the rice, if cooked earlier, before combining with other ingredients.

*SHOP SMART, PREP SMART, COOK SMART TIPS:

* We like the medium grain brown rice, which is a bit "stickier" than long-grain.
* If you haven't had a good experience cooking brown rice in the past, use a rice cooker or boiling brown rice just like pasta. Add 1-2 cups of rinsed brown rice to a large pot of boiling water, stirring it once, cooking it uncovered for 30 minutes, then draining it for 15 seconds, adding it back to the pot and putting the lid on to allow it to steam (off the heat) for a few minutes.
* I typically make a big pot of rice over the weekend and then we have it for this recipe, as well as our Weeknight Un-Fried Rice pg94.

RECIPE USED IN THESE BARS:

Crazy Salad Foodie Bar

Pasta Foodie Bar

*SHOP SMART, PREP SMART, COOK SMART TIP:

* I always keep bread in the freezer, as it tends to mold at room temperature so quickly! I also keep a zip-top bag in the freezer for the "heels/ends" of each loaf, so that I will be ready to make croutons whenever I need to.

The Nutrition Professor's Homemade Croutons

Homemade croutons can be a delicious component of any salad. Be sure to make these croutons whenever you accumulate some "bread heels/ends" in the freezer and have the oven on for another purpose. They will last for weeks in an airtight container on the counter or in your pantry (or for even longer, in the freezer).

INGREDIENTS

100% whole grain bread (heels/ends) with lots of nuts/seeds on the crust

Granulated garlic (powder), to taste

Italian Seasoning pg278, to taste

Black pepper, a sprinkle

PROCEDURE

1. Cut the bread into small, uniform cubes and put into a clean produce bag (or empty bread bag).

2. Add the garlic powder, Italian Seasoning and black pepper. Shake well to coat the bread.

3. Pour contents of bag on to a baking sheet lined with parchment paper and bake at 325°F-350°F until very crisp and lightly brown.

4. Check them after 10 minutes and then every few minutes, stirring the croutons for even browning. They need to be completely dry (crispy), but you do not want them to burn!

RECIPE USED IN THESE BARS:

Pizza Foodie Bar
Pasta Foodie Bar
Dilla Foodie Bar

*SHOP SMART, PREP SMART, COOK SMART TIPS:

* When fresh tomatoes are not in season, look for organic jarred tomatoes in shelf-stable, cardboard box-type packaging.
* Using a box grater to grate the onion (instead of chopping it) has been shown to help "soften" the onion flavor (source: America's Test Kitchen).
* To maximize the amazing power of garlic's phytonutrients, be sure to press it (through a garlic press) or chop it well and let it sit for at least 10 minutes before adding heat or acid (e.g. cooking with onions and adding tomatoes in this recipe).

Quick Tomato Sauce

When you taste this tomato sauce, you might think that it had been simmering on the stove for hours, not 10 minutes! It is a delicious staple that you can use for pasta, pizza, lasagna, stuffed shells, Pizza-dillas pg90 and more! It also freezes well, so when tomato season is peaking, make several batches!

INGREDIENTS

28 oz tomatoes, canned, crushed* (OR ~5 cups ripe cherry tomatoes, cut into quarters)

¼ cup red onion, grated on a box grater*

¼ teaspoon oregano, dried

2 teaspoon dried basil or 2 Tablespoons fresh basil

¼-½ teaspoon salt (based on taste preferences)

2 garlic cloves, pressed/minced*

¼ teaspoon sugar (date/coconut sugar)

PROCEDURE

1. Warm a large sauté pan over medium to medium-high heat, add red onion and let brown (caramelize) without stirring. As the color develops, stir to prevent burning, adding a Tablespoon or two of water, if needed.

2. When onions are golden, add garlic, oregano, salt and basil (if using dried basil). Stir regularly to avoid burning (burnt garlic is very bitter!) for 30 seconds.

3. Add the tomatoes and date sugar, increase heat to high and bring to a boil. Lower heat to medium-low and simmer for ~10 minutes, until thickened. Puree in standard blender or with immersion blender if smooth texture is desired.

4. If using fresh basil, stir in after sauce has been taken off the heat.

RECIPE USED IN THESE BARS:

Pizza Foodie Bar
Pasta Foodie Bar

*SHOP SMART, PREP SMART, COOK SMART TIPS:

* Silken tofu is sold in paper cartons, similar to a "juice box" – keep at room temp in your pantry, until you are ready to open the package and get cooking! (Look for organic/non-GMO)
* If you have a deep stock pot, you can use a metal colander or sieve to steam the veggies right above the pasta water (not touching the water).
* In addition to the steamed veggies, for a **punch of added flavor,** try some of our favorite pasta mix-ins: sun-dried tomatoes, garlic mushrooms, olives, artichoke hearts, and scallions.
* You can also stir in a few Tablespoons of Quick Tomato Sauce pg256 for a creamy tomato sauce!

Creamy Pasta Sauce

This pasta sauce is so creamy that you will swear it is dairy-based and full of fat! It whips up in even less time than it takes to boil the pasta! Make the sauce, then steam your favorite veggie (broccoli, asparagus, cauliflower, chopped kale, chard and/or collards, peas, zucchini) while the pasta cooks. Sprinkle your delicious pasta dish with Cheezy Parm pg272 for an incredibly tasty meal!

INGREDIENTS

12.3 ounces firm silken* tofu, drained (but not pressed)

1-2 garlic cloves* (2 cloves if you LOVE garlic – use roasted garlic pg229 for a milder version)

1 ½ teaspoons dried parsley

1 ½ teaspoons dried basil (or your favorite herb)

¼ teaspoon smoked paprika

½ teaspoon salt

⅓ cup vegetable broth (approximately)

For Serving:

Whole grain pasta

Favorite vegetables – steamed (see ideas above)

Flavor-punch mix-ins

Cheezy Parm pg272

PROCEDURE

1. Combine all sauce ingredients in a blender or food processor and combine until smooth.

2. Heat the sauce on medium-low, until warm through, being careful not to boil, as it will get too thick.

3. Keep leftover sauce tightly covered in the fridge for a week, though I bet that it will be eaten up in just a few days!

Recipe adapted by The Nutrition Professor from www.food.com

*SHOP SMART, PREP SMART, COOK SMART TIPS:

* Use your favorite white bean! I often cook up a whole pound and freeze what I don't use right away: 1 ½ cups of beans per zip-top bag.
* Flavor boosts for the spread: red chili flakes, finely diced olives, finely chopped parsley, sun-dried tomatoes, fresh garlic – proceed with caution when it comes to the amount of fresh garlic, as the flavor will intensify over time (esp. overnight)!

RECIPE USED IN THESE BARS:

Mediterranean Fajita Foodie Bar

Dilla Foodie Bar

Mediterranean Spread

Get creative with this delicious recipe! Spread on whole grain toasted bruschetta and top with sun-dried tomatoes and olive tapenade, in a whole wheat pita with fresh veggies (grated carrot, thinly sliced cucumbers and tomatoes and a spoon of olive tapenade pg262), in a whole grain wrap with grilled veggies and a splash of balsamic vinegar in Greek Fajitas pg60, or as an alternative to hummus. It even freezes perfectly in small containers! Just thaw in the refrigerator overnight and you'll be ready to go!

INGREDIENTS

1 ½ cups of cooked white beans*

~10 cloves of Roasted Garlic pg228

1 ½ teaspoons of Italian Seasoning pg278

¼ teaspoon salt (optional – to taste)

Flavor boosts*

1-3 Tablespoons fresh lemon juice or veggie broth (only add liquid if spread is too thick)

PROCEDURE

1. Combine all ingredients, except lemon juice or broth, in food processor and puree until texture is smooth and creamy, adding a splash at a time of the lemon juice/broth, if too stiff.

2. If you are lucky enough to have any leftover spread, the flavor will only improve with time, and it will be good for several days in the fridge or for months, if frozen!

*SHOP SMART, PREP SMART, COOK SMART TIPS:

* I keep a jar of capers in my pantry for a variety of recipes, including this one and Lemony Caesar-ish Salad Dressing pg120. Since I am very careful to use a clean spoon when dipping into the jar in the fridge, they will last for several months.

* Be sure to zest citrus fruits BEFORE cutting them into pieces to squeeze the juice. A microplane is my favorite zesting tool, and we want the zest, as it may prevent skin cancer!

* To maximize the amazing power of garlic's phytonutrients, be sure to press it (through a garlic press) or chop it well and let it sit for at least 10 minutes before adding it to the tapenade, since it contains vinegar and lemon juice (acids).

* I always keep a bag of walnuts in the freezer (to extend their life), and so that I have them when I need them.

Black and Green Olive Tapenade

This is a fun spread for raw or lightly steamed veggies or crispy whole grain crackers, especially when served side by side with my Power Pesto pg130. It makes a flavorful addition to a sandwich or pizza, and a little goes a long way. A thin layer can take the place of mayo, and little spoonfuls can be dropped on top of the sauce layer, before adding greens to your pizza creation (Pizza Foodie Bar pg66 or Thin-Crust Kale Pizza pg68).

INGREDIENTS

¼ cup capers*, drained (jarred)

1 cup black olives

½ cup green olives, stuffed with pimento or garlic

½ teaspoon lemon zest* (optional)

1-2 teaspoons lemon juice

1 teaspoon red wine vinegar

1 small garlic clove, pressed/minced* or 3-4 gloves roasted garlic pg228

⅛ teaspoon thyme, dried

⅛ teaspoon black pepper, ground

2 Tablespoons roasted red pepper, jarred (optional)

1 Tablespoon walnuts* (optional)

4 teaspoons water (as needed to keep contents moving in food processor)

PROCEDURE

1. Press/mince garlic and set aside while gathering the rest of the ingredients.

2. Combine all ingredients in food processor and process until well combined and relatively smooth, (no big chunks).

3. Will keep well in an airtight storage container in the back of the fridge for at least a week.

Delisa's Mayo

Delisa Renideo is a wonderful woman, and kindred spirit, who is helping people become better versions of themselves everyday. She is based in Wasilla, Alaska, an hour outside of Anchorage and is well known for leading fantastic cooking demonstrations and life-changing classes!

You won't believe that this wonderfully creamy mayo is oil-free!

INGREDIENTS

1 – 12.3 ounce package firm or extra-firm silken tofu

½-¾ teaspoon salt

¾ teaspoon onion powder

½ teaspoon garlic powder

½ teaspoon coconut sugar or date sugar

2 teaspoons dijon mustard

1 Tablespoon apple cider vinegar

2 Tablespoons raw cashews (optional, but adds richness)

PROCEDURE

Combine all ingredients in a blender and process until completely smooth. Chill thoroughly before using.

Recipe printed with permission by Delisa Renideo www.yestolifesolution.com

RECIPE USED IN THESE BARS:

Burrito Bowl Foodie Bar
Loaded Potato Foodie Bar
Nacho Foodie Bar
Dilla Foodie Bar

*SHOP SMART, PREP SMART, COOK SMART TIPS:

* Uncooked, old-fashioned, or "5-min" dry oatmeal works great – do not use steel cut oats
* Be sure to buy nutritional yeast (do not use Brewer's Yeast or Active Yeast, the type used for making bread).
* This sauce can also be frozen. Once thawed, the sauce will separate, but will come back together when gently heated in a saucepan while whisking.

Our Favorite "Cheezie" Sauce

This cheese sauce is adored by my son and tastes delicious on everything from baked potatoes with broccoli pg74 to nachos pg84 (be sure to make the Mexican Quinoa pg248 or Califlower Lentil Filling pg220 for your nachos)!

INGREDIENTS

6 Tablespoons raw cashews

6 Tablespoons raw sunflower seeds

6 Tablespoons rolled oats*

6 Tablespoons nutritional yeast*

3 Tablespoons lemon juice (fresh squeezed is best)

3 Tablespoons cornstarch or arrowroot

1 red bell pepper (stem, seeds and ribs removed) – cut into large chunks

1 ½ teaspoons maple syrup or Date Syrup pg295

1 ½ teaspoons onion powder

½ teaspoon smoked paprika

½ teaspoon granulated garlic powder (or 1 small clove fresh garlic)

2 teaspoons salt (or less - to taste)

4 cups water, divided (1 cup & 3 cups)

PROCEDURE

1. Soak the sunflower seeds and cashews in one cup of the water for 20 minutes to overnight in refrigerator.

2. Add the seeds, nuts, soaking liquid, and the remainder of the ingredients (including the additional 3 cups of water) to a very powerful blender (Vita-Mix/Blendtec/ OmniBlend) and puree until silky smooth.

3. Transfer mixture to a saucepan and bring to a gradual boil, whisking frequently to avoid burning the bottom.

4. Keep whisking, but reduce heat and simmer until the desired thickness has been achieved, ~15 minutes.

5. Sauce will thicken significantly once cooled in the fridge, so plan to whisk a substantial amount of water into each portion that you reheat.

Recipe slightly adapted by The Nutrition Professor from I Love Veggies, by Mary Bernt.

RECIPE USED IN THESE BARS:

Mediterranean Fajita Foodie Bar

Pizza Foodie Bar

Pasta Foodie Bar

*SHOP SMART, PREP SMART, COOK SMART TIPS:

* Look for extra-firm organic tofu packaged in water. In preparation for making this recipe, remove the tofu from the plastic container, wrap it in a clean dish towel and press out extra liquid by squeezing tightly (don't worry about crushing the tofu, as it will need to be crumbled when being added to the food processor. You can also "drain" the towel wrapped tofu by setting it on the sink under a weighted baking tray for ~10-30 minutes.)
* If using fresh basil, double the amount (1-1 ½ Tablespoons)
* Store all nuts in the freezer to help maximize shelf life. Vacuum sealing is very effective, too!
* To maximize the amazing power of garlic's phytonutrients, be sure to press it (through a garlic press) or chop it well and let it sit for at least 10 minutes before adding heat or acid (e.g. lemon juice in this recipe).

Ricotta Cheeze

This alternative to traditional ricotta cheese has 90% less saturated fat and is cholesterol free. It can be used in a variety of savory recipes including lasagna, ravioli, stuffed pasta sheets, filo appetizers and even on pizza!

INGREDIENTS

14 oz organic, extra-firm tofu, drained and crumbled*

2 teaspoons dried basil*

1 teaspoon Italian Seasoning (store-bought or use my recipe pg278)

2 Tablespoons fresh parsley, minced (optional)

¼-½ teaspoon salt (based on taste preferences)

1 garlic clove, pressed/minced*

3-4 Tablespoons lemon juice

¼ cup cashews, raw,* soaked overnight (optional)

PROCEDURE

1. In a food processor, blend together the cashews, lemon juice and garlic until a thick, creamy paste forms.

2. Add the crumbled tofu, basil, Italian Seasoning, salt and parsley (if using) and process until well blended. Add a Tablespoon of water if mixture is too thick.

    If you don't have a food processor, you can easily make this recipe if you skip the cashews (unless you don't mind chunky texture). Simply crumble the tofu into a large mixing bowl and mash it with a long-tined fork. Then add the lemon juice, basil, Italian Seasoning, garlic, finely minced parsley and salt. Stir/mash until combined well.

RECIPE USED IN THESE BARS:

**Mediterranean Fajita
Foodie Bar**

Pizza Foodie Bar

Crazy Salad Foodie Bar

Pasta Foodie Bar

Dilla Foodie Bar

*SHOP SMART, PREP SMART, COOK SMART TIPS:

* If I am making some Italian food, I will often use half of the block of tofu for this feta cheeze recipe and the other for my Ricotta Cheeze pg268.
* Miso is a fermented product (think yummy miso soup), most commonly available in the refrigerated section of the produce area in the grocery store. Many products use soybeans and rice or barley, but there are also some alternatives if you are allergic to soy, including chickpea miso (some brands are also gluten-free).
* Nutritional yeast is sold as flakes or powder, often in the bulk aisle of supermarkets. It is a deactivated form of yeast grown on sugarcane or beet molasses, and is VERY different from active yeast used in bread-making or brewer's yeast, and cannot be used as a substitute for either. Nutritional yeast provides a cheesy, nutty flavor.
* To maximize the amazing power of garlic's phytonutrients, be sure to press it (through a garlic press) or chop it well and let it sit for at least 10 minutes before adding it to the feta marinade, since it contains vinegar and lemon juice (acids).

Feta Cheeze

While traditional feta cheese is made from animal milk – typically sheep's or goat's milk, this version is free of animal products and cholesterol, will be ready in a few minutes and has a great flavor. Use it as you would any salty condiment, as a little crumble on your salad pg70, pizza pg66 or humm-adilla pg88 will go a long way!

INGREDIENTS

~8 oz of extra firm tofu* (water packed)*

2 teaspoons water

2 teaspoons yellow miso paste*

2 Tablespoons red wine vinegar

¼ teaspoon lemon zest* + 2 teaspoons lemon juice

⅛ teaspoon black pepper, ground

2 teaspoons Italian Seasoning (store bought – or my recipe pg278)

¼ teaspoon salt (based on taste preference)

¼-½ teaspoon granulated garlic powder or ½ fresh clove of garlic (optional)

1 Tablespoon nutritional yeast* (optional)

PROCEDURE

1. Drain and rinse the tofu, wrap in paper towels or a clean dish cloth and squeeze to remove excess liquid. Don't worry about breaking up the tofu, as you will need to crumble it next.

2. Using a long tined fork, mash the tofu to resemble feta cheese crumbles.

3. If you are using fresh garlic, press the garlic and let it sit for 10 minutes while you assemble the other ingredients.

4. In a medium sized bowl, combine the water, miso, vinegar, lemon zest and juice, pepper, Italian Seasoning, salt and nutritional yeast (if using).

5. Add the crumbled tofu and mix well. Taste and adjust seasonings, if needed.

6. The flavors will continue to develop with time, and it will store well in the refrigerator for several days.

Recipe adapted by The Nutrition Professor from www.sheknows.com (Brianna Martinez)

Cheezy Parm

Sprinkle this delicious topping on pasta dishes, pizza, salads, grain dishes, or more! Use it on any dish that you would normally dust with Parmesan or Romano cheese. Since it lasts for a long time in the fridge or freezer, you can always have it on hand!

INGREDIENTS

⅔ cup nutritional yeast

½ cup raw almonds, cashews or walnuts

¼ teaspoon garlic powder

¼ teaspoon onion powder

¼ teaspoon lemon zest

¼-½ teaspoon salt (optional)

PROCEDURE

1. Put all the ingredients into a standing blender or food processor and pulse until very fine and crumbly.

2. **Don't over-process**, as it will turn into a paste. Simply pulse until the nuts are finely chopped.

3. You can double the recipe, as the mixture will store in the refrigerator for at least a month, or in the freezer for several months.

Adapted by The Nutrition Professor from http://plantpoweredkitchen.com

*SHOP SMART, PREP SMART, COOK SMART TIP:

*   When you buy nutritional yeast, be sure that you are not buying baker's yeast or brewer's yeast.
*   While health food stores carry nutritional yeast, it can also be found in the bulk bins at many grocery stores.

274

Brazil Nut Parm

Here is another option for sprinkling on pasta or other recipes (a little goes a long way – see important information about not getting too much selenium). The garlic can get intense as days pass, so be ready for a little punch of flavor! Studies have linked eating four Brazil nuts a month to lowering "bad" cholesterol! Now, coming from an Italian family whose members were known to make little "piles" of Romano cheese on empty dinner plates disappear, don't overdo it with Brazil nuts (or this Brazil Nut Parm), as the nuts are a very rich source of selenium and can cause a toxicity.*

INGREDIENTS

6 raw Brazil nuts

1 garlic clove, small

¼ teaspoon salt (optional)

¼ teaspoon lemon zest (optional)

Optional – 10 walnut halves (to "dilute" the selenium from the Brazil nuts and increase the quantity)

Optional – 2 teaspoons nutritional yeast

PROCEDURE

Put all the ingredients into a mini-chopper or small food processor and pulse until crumbly, but not a paste (which will happen quickly, so stay focused on this task).

Adapted by The Nutrition Professor from class given by Adam Lovelace.

*SHOP SMART, PREP SMART, COOK SMART TIPS:

* Each brazil nut provides ~90 mcg of selenium, which has a recommended daily intake of 55 mcg and a tolerable upper level of 400 mcg per day.
* When you buy nutritional yeast, be sure that you are not buying baker's yeast or brewer's yeast. Look for "nutritional yeast" – which can be found packaged as well as in the bulk bins at many supermarkets.

RECIPE USED IN THESE BARS:

Kale Chip Foodie Bar
Baked Chip Foodie Bar
Guacamole Foodie Bar
Salsa Foodie Bar

Austin's Smoky Spice Blend

My son developed this salt-free spice blend when we were experimenting with savory soup recipes. You'll probably want to double or triple the recipe, since it is so versatile. This spice blend can be tossed with veggies to roast or grill, makes a great topping for homemade tortilla chips (Mia's 1-2-3 Easy Tortilla Chips pg154), and can season Mexican Quinoa pg248, soups, taco fillings, scrambles and more! Look it up in the Index for more great recipes and Foodie Bars that use it!

INGREDIENTS

2 teaspoons coriander, ground

½ teaspoon black pepper, ground

1 teaspoon oregano, dried leaves

1 teaspoon smoked* paprika

½-1 teaspoon cayenne* pepper, ground

1 teaspoon granulated garlic powder*

PROCEDURE

Combine all ingredients in a medium sized bowl and mix well. Kept in a small air-tight container, this spice blend will last for at least a few months.

*SHOP SMART, PREP SMART, COOK SMART TIPS:

* Be sure to buy SMOKED paprika, not "regular" paprika, as they taste completely different
* Cayenne can be quite spicy on the tongue, and it is much easier to fix a "not enough spice" problem, than a "my lips are burning off and my mouth/throat is on fire" problem, so start with a small amount of cayenne and work up slowly!
* Be sure to use granulated garlic (dry powder), NOT garlic salt!

The Nutrition Professor!

SHOP SMART • COOK SMART
EAT SMART

RECIPE USED IN THESE BARS:

**Mediterranean Fajita
Foodie Bar**

**Salad Dressing (Shaken)
Foodie Bar**

Pesto Foodie Bar

Kale Chip Foodie Bar

Hummus Foodie Bar

Homemade Italian Seasoning

This Italian Seasoning is wonderfully versatile, and can be adjusted to your taste preferences. Enjoy adding it to your pasta or pizza sauce, sprinkle it on sandwiches and in wraps, incorporate it into your salad dressings and soups, toss veggies with it before or after roasting or grilling, add it to steaming water for artichokes, sprinkle it on your homemade veggie pizza, stir into grain and bean salads or dishes that combine greens and beans, in a stuffing for peppers, mushrooms or zucchini, on Homemade Croutons pg254 or in Mediterranean Spread pg260. Look it up in the Index for more great ideas for recipes and Foodie Bars which use this seasoning!

INGREDIENTS

½ cup dried oregano

½ cup dried basil

¼ cup dried rosemary

¼ cup dried marjoram

¼ cup dried thyme

¼ cup dried sage

2 Tablespoons dried granulated/minced garlic*

PROCEDURE

Combine all ingredients and store in an air-tight container in a cool dark cabinet (away from the oven).

*SHOP SMART, PREP SMART, COOK SMART TIPS:

* Store all dried herbs, spices and blends in a dark cabinet away from your stove and dishwasher, as you don't want to subject them to big shifts in temperature.
* Use these flavor enhancers often, as the herbs and spices will lose their potency when kept in the pantry for months and months.
* Be sure to purchase granulated garlic or dried minced garlic, not garlic salt!

RECIPE USED IN THESE BARS:

Baked Chip Foodie Bar
Guacamole Foodie Bar
Salsa Foodie Bar

Savory Spice Blend

I developed this blend when I wanted to season some homemade pita chips pg156. Play around with the amounts of each of the ingredients to come up with a great balance of flavors for you.

INGREDIENTS

2 teaspoons cumin, ground

1 teaspoon coriander, ground

1 teaspoon granulated garlic powder*

½ teaspoon black pepper, ground

1 teaspoon oregano, dried leaves

½ teaspoon smoked* paprika

¼ teaspoon cayenne* pepper

pinch of salt (optional)

PROCEDURE

Combine all ingredients in a medium sized bowl and mix well. Kept in a small air-tight container, this spice blend will last for at least a few months in a cool, dark cabinet.

*SHOP SMART, PREP SMART, COOK SMART TIPS:

* Be sure to buy SMOKED paprika, not "regular" paprika, as they taste completely different
* Cayenne can be quite spicy on the tongue, and it is much easier to fix a "not enough spice" problem, than a "my lips are burning off and my mouth/throat is on fire" problem, so start with a small amount of cayenne and work up slowly!
* Be sure to use granulated garlic (dry powder), NOT garlic salt!

RECIPE USED IN THESE BARS:

Oatmeal Foodie Bar

Granola Foodie Bar

Banana Bread Snack Cake
Foodie Bar

Oatmeal Cookie Foodie
Bar

Chai Spice Blend

Making your own spice mixes is easy and can save you money!

This Chai Spice Blend can be substituted for cinnamon in nearly every recipe, and enjoyed in oatmeal pg38 & pg42, your favorite homemade granola pg46, sprinkled on roasted winter squash (slices or pureed), in a smoothie, on cereal, in a fruit crisp, on freshly fruit slices (apples, pears, persimmons, citrus), in pancakes, cookies, muffins, or French toast, on a baked sweet potato or stirred into warmed almond or soy milk.

INGREDIENTS

1 teaspoon allspice

1 teaspoon cardamom, ground*

1 teaspoon cinnamon, Ceylon

1 teaspoon coriander

½ teaspoon black pepper*

½ teaspoon nutmeg

½ teaspoon turmeric*

PROCEDURE

Combine ingredients in an air-tight container and shake to mix well. Keep in an air tight container that is front and center in your spice cabinet, so that you use it often.

*SHOP SMART, PREP SMART, COOK SMART TIPS:

* This blend is especially wonderful, as the black pepper improves your body's ability to absorb turmeric by as much as 2000%!
* I always quadruple the recipe when I make this blend because I use it so often!
* Get accustomed to using herbs and spices everyday, they won't "last" forever. Especially since those which are ground, lose their potency over time.
* Ceylon Cinnamon is your best choice when it comes to health-promoting potential.

RECIPE USED IN THESE BARS:

Oatmeal Foodie Bar

Granola Foodie Bar

Banana Bread Snack Cake
Foodie Bar

Granola Foodie Bar

Oatmeal Cookie Foodie
Bar

Pumpkin Pie Spice

This spice blend can be substituted for cinnamon in nearly every recipe! I love it sprinkled on baked winter squash, sweet potatoes, oatmeal pg38, in oatmeal cookies pg204, pancakes, chia pudding and even on cereal or stirred into warmed almond or soy milk.

INGREDIENTS

4 teaspoons cinnamon, Ceylon

1 teaspoon ground ginger

½ teaspoon ground nutmeg

½ teaspoon ground cloves

PROCEDURE

Combine all of the ingredients and mix well.

*SHOP SMART, PREP SMART, COOK SMART TIPS:

* Ceylon cinnamon is available online and is the best choice, health-wise!
* I typically double or quadruple the recipe, so that I have enough on hand.
* Keep spice mixes in air-tight containers and use them often, as they amp up the flavors of your food and are packed with antioxidant power to keep you at your best from the inside out!

RECIPE USED IN THESE BARS:

Breakwich Foodie Bar
Fruit Skewers Foodie Bar
Dessert Nacho Foodie Bar

*SHOP SMART, PREP SMART, COOK SMART TIPS:

* Be sure to double check that you have removed the pit from each of the dates. If you miss one, it will definitely ruin your sauce, and maybe even your blender!
* While any cooked bean will work, black beans are best due to their color.

T's Dreamy Chocolate Sauce

Developing this recipe was so exciting, as it was "love at first bite" for my kids! Their smiles grew bigger as they considered all of the possibilities! This chocolate sauce is truly "dreamy" for many reasons! Not only is it crazy delicious, but it is a cinch to whip up with just a handful of ingredients that you probably already have on hand, but never realized worked so well together and were energy boosters! While this stellar sauce would last the in fridge for a few days, my guess is that it will vanish pretty quickly! Try it as a topping for homemade pancakes or waffles, drizzle it into a whole grain tortilla or crepe filled with fresh fruit, add it to oatmeal with sliced banana and walnuts or make Dessert Nachos pg200!

INGREDIENTS

5 Medjool dates (pits* removed, soaked in ¾ cup water)

1 Tablespoon cashews (can soak with the dates) or raw sunflower seeds

2 Tablespoons unsweetened cocoa/cacao powder

½ cup cooked black beans*

¼ teaspoon cinnamon

½ teaspoon vanilla

Extra water on hand to add to during blending

PROCEDURE

1. In a high-powered blender (e.g. Vitamix or Blendtec), combine all of the ingredients, including the soaking water for the dates, and blend until silky smooth.

2. Add extra water, a Tablespoon or so at a time, (up to ~5 Tablespoons total), to achieve the right consistency, (a semi-thick sauce rather than a stiff dip).

3. Store in a squeeze bottle, in the back of the fridge.

RECIPE USED IN THESE BARS:

Breakwich Foodie Bar
Fruit Skewers Foodie Bar
Dessert Nacho Foodie Bar

*SHOP SMART, PREP SMART, COOK SMART TIPS:

* This is a perfect recipe to double or triple if you have a big family, as it will be gone in NO TIME!
* Be sure to double check that you have removed the pit from each of the dates. If you miss one, it will definitely ruin your sauce, and maybe even your blender!
* Experiment with other spices, as you may enjoy using Pumpkin Pie Spice pg284 or Chai Spice Blend pg282, in place of the cinnamon.

Date Night Caramel Sauce

You won't want to reserve this sauce for date night, as it is a delectable topping for homemade pancakes, waffles and whole grain toast with your favorite nut butter. We like it drizzled into a whole grain tortilla or crepe filled with fresh fruit, on oatmeal pg50 with sliced banana and walnuts or on Mom's Apple Berry Nachos pg202. Have fun getting creative with it!

INGREDIENTS

5 Medjool dates (pits* removed, soaked in ½ cup water – reserve water)

1 Tablespoon cashews (can soak with the dates) or raw sunflower seeds

½ cup water (used to soak the dates & cashews)

½ apple, cored, but unpeeled

½ -1 teaspoon vanilla

¼ teaspoon cinnamon* (optional)

Extra water on hand to add to during blending

PROCEDURE

1. In a high-powered blender (e.g. Vitamix or Blendtec), combine all of the ingredients, including the soaking water for the dates, and blend until silky smooth.

2. Add extra water, a Tablespoon at a time, to achieve the desired consistency (semi-thick sauce).

3. Store in a squeeze bottle, in the back of the fridge.

RECIPE USED IN THESE BARS:

Breakwich Foodie Bar
Fruit Skewers Foodie Bar
Dessert Nacho Foodie Bar

*SHOP SMART, PREP SMART, COOK SMART TIPS:

* This is a perfect recipe to double or triple so that you have it on hand to drizzle!
* Be sure to double check that you have removed the pit from each of the dates. If you miss one, it will definitely ruin your sauce, and maybe even your blender!
* Experiment with other citrus fruits. Orange and lime are also great with all varieties of berries!

Dazzle-Berry Sauce

While this sauce is simple to make, it will add pizzaz to many different dishes, from breakfast to dessert! Drizzle on homemade pancakes or waffles, into a whole grain tortilla or crepe filled with fresh fruit, add it to oatmeal with sliced banana and walnuts or make Dessert Nachos pg198 with "chips" made from thin slices of fresh apple or pineapple.

INGREDIENTS

5 Medjool dates (pits* removed, soaked in ½ cup water)

1 Tablespoon cashews (can soak with the dates) or raw sunflower seeds

½ cup blackberries, blueberries, raspberries (or mixture)

¼ teaspoon cinnamon

½ teaspoon vanilla

½-1 teaspoon lemon* zest

Extra water on hand to add to during blending

PROCEDURE

1. In a high-powered blender (e.g. Vitamix or Blendtec), combine all of the ingredients, including the soaking water for the dates, and blend until silky smooth.

2. Add extra water, a Tablespoon at a time, to achieve the desired consistency (semi-thick sauce).

3. Store in a squeeze bottle, in the back of the fridge.

RECIPE USED IN THESE BARS:

Breakwich Foodie Bar
Fruit Skewers Foodie Bar
Dessert Nacho Foodie Bar

*SHOP SMART, PREP SMART, COOK SMART TIPS:

* Frozen mango is typically bursting with flavor as it isn't picked until it is perfectly ripe and then frozen right away. I always keep some in my freezer and the rest of the ingredients on hand, as I have been surprised by how quickly this sauce disappears!

* Be sure to double check that you have removed the pit from each of the dates. If you miss one, it will definitely ruin your sauce, and maybe even your blender!

Sweet Mango Lime Sauce

While this tasty sauce can be made in a few minutes with minimal effort, be prepared to be impressed as it can transform pancakes, waffles, fresh fruit salad, sweet crêpes and even hot cereal into a delicious work of art! I love it drizzled on thinly sliced apples, kiwi slices, and fresh pineapple cut into thin planks as a fun version of Dessert Nachos pg198. Don't forget to add a sprinkle of cayenne pepper.

INGREDIENTS

5 Medjool dates (pits* removed, soaked in ¾ cup water)

1 cup of mango chunks, fresh or slightly thawed from frozen*

½ cup white beans, cooked

1 Tablespoon unsweetened coconut, toasted (optional)

¼ teaspoon ginger, powdered

¼ to ½ teaspoon lime* zest

Extra water on hand to add to during blending

PROCEDURE

1. In a high-powered blender (e.g. Vitamix or Blendtec), combine all of the ingredients, including the soaking water for the dates, and blend until silky smooth.

2. Add extra water, 1-2 Tablespoons at a time, to achieve the desired consistency (semi-thick sauce).

3. Store in a squeeze bottle, in the back of the fridge.

RECIPE USED IN THESE BARS:

Granola Foodie Bar
Breakwich Foodie Bar
**Salad Dressing (Shaken)
Foodie Bar**
**Salad Dressing (Blended)
Foodie Bar**
Kale Chip Foodie Bar

The Nutrition Professor's Date Syrup

I have started making a weekly batch of this date syrup for the fridge. That way, my family can use it in place of maple syrup, which provides 4 times the calories of date syrup!

INGREDIENTS

10 pitted (Medjool) dates, pitted and coarsely chopped*

1 ½ cups of water

½ teaspoon of vanilla (or extract of your choice, using more to taste)

¾ teaspoon of cinnamon

PROCEDURE

1. Combine ingredients in a powerful blender until very smooth, adding more water until the desired thickness is achieved.

2. We like our syrup a bit thick, as it is easier to keep in the shallow nooks and crannies of our homemade waffles!

*SHOP SMART, PREP SMART, COOK SMART TIPS:

* Double check to be sure that you have removed all of the pits, as they will ruin the syrup and maybe even your blender!
* If the dates you use are a bit hard, let the ingredients sit in the blender for 15-30 minutes so the dates can soften before blending.
* Store date syrup in a squeeze bottle in the back of the fridge and give it a good shake before using.

ACKNOWLEDGMENTS

This cookbook has been a long time coming, as I have LOVED working with ingredients and recipes since I was young. T's Cinnamon Toast, was the first recipe that I wrote down, when I was around 6 years old and I have been collecting cookbooks ever since! I would like to honor both of my grand-mothers – my Nonna and my Gram Crax, with this effort. While I had the wonderful experience of being able to cook with them and for them, I only wish they could have thumbed through these pages.

I have so many people to acknowledge, as it took a village to get The Foodie Bar™ Way into your hands! This book wouldn't be nearly as well organized, or as gorgeous, if it wasn't for Stephanie Faiferek, graphic and web designer extraordinaire! Not only is my husband Scot my rock of unwavering support, but he also photographed many of my recipes, along with my dear friend, and photography professor, Kathryn Mayo. My children, Austin and Mia, are my light, they give me so much joy! I especially love cooking together and learning how they are "plant-based ambassadors of health" for others kids around them. My parents, Tony and Judi Spadaro, have always provided me with unconditional love and support. I am thrilled that they are healthier than ever, an inspiration to their friends and a local Complete Health Improvement Program (CHIP) in Meadow Vista, as they, too, are thriving on plant-based whole foods and riding their motorcycles, anywhere and everywhere! I am so lucky to have my sister, Misty Platt, in my life! She has always believed in me and even though our lives are so busy, our deep connection is unshak-able. She and my brother-in-law, Joe, have four amazing children, Robyn, Ethan, Kate and Allie Rose, all of whom have loved being "recipe taste tes-ters" through the years! Melissa Stone designed the caricature in my logo, which always brings a smile to my face! Jenni Frisk and Nancy Reich, are my faithful exercise buddies who have been ever so patient, as I contemplated every step on this journey.

My heart is full with gratitude for so many people who have been helpful and supportive: Dana Wassmer, Makayla Hopkins, Doug Winter, Jessica Lynn Martinez, Camille Moreno, Tracy Sellers, Scott Monaco, Clark Driftmier, Chip and Bobbie Morris, Evelyn Ruehr, Tammy McGeorge, Delisa and Charlie Renideo, Brenda Rea, Jill Nussinow, Lani Muelrath, Laurie Cotulla, Nancy Coughlin, Kirk Evans, Veronica Lopez, Alex Badolian, Rubina Gulati, Cori Burns, Amy Avalos, Kristie West, Bob Johnson, Cheryl Douglas, Debbie Lucus, Linda Middlesworth, Christie Hagenburger, Joann and Jim Helmich, Robin Withrow-Wong, Vivienne Gerard, Ashley Mason, Rochell May, Amy Myrdal Miller, Scott Miller, Barbara Nuss, Kaye Carpenter, Alena Basurto, Kathy Scheffer, Rittu Hans, Fred Deneke, Jim Eastman, Alex Casareno, Michelle Barkley, Barbara Boyer, Anita Robbins, Michelle Segar, Adina Magallon and our CRC TOP Club (Thrive on Plants).

Special mention to some of the rockstars of the plant-based world, who inspire me and enable me to share phenomenal research, compelling insights and delicious recipe ideas with my students and the world: Dr. Michael Greger, Dr. John and Mary McDougall, Dr. Neal Barnard, Dr. Caldwell Esselstyn, T. Colin Campbell, Dr. Doug Lisle, Dr. Joel Fuhrman, Dr. Don Forrester, Dr. Robert Ostfeld, Dr. Richard Oppenlander, Dr. Jami Dulaney, Dr. Garth Davis, Cathy Fisher, Isa Chandra Moskowitz, Caryn Hartglass, Hal Elrod, Jeff Sanders, Rich Roll, John Pierre, Howard Jacobsen, Victoria Moran, Dino Sarma, John Wiener, Mioyoko Schinner, Chad Sarno and Jon Tedd.

INDEX